The Story of the Christ

THE STORY
OF THE CHRIST

Scot McKnight

Gospel abridgement by Philip Law

Baker Academic
Grand Rapids, Michigan

© 2006 by Scot McKnight

Published by Baker Academic
a division of Baker Publishing Group
P.O. Box 6287, Grand Rapids, MI 49516-6287
www.bakeracademic.com

Printed in Great Britain

Library of Congress Cataloging-in-Publication Data is on file at the
Library of Congress, Washington, DC.

CONTENTS

Part One: Looking at Jesus from the Outside

1 What Are the Gospels, and
   Where Did They Come From?   3
2 What Was Religion Like at the Time of Jesus?   12
3 What Were the Main Themes of Jesus' Teaching?   22
4 What Was Jesus Like?   45

Part Two: The Story of the Christ

   Prologue   64
1 Birth and Early Years   65
2 Baptism and Early Ministry   74
3 The Sermon on the Mount   93
4 Healings and Teachings   101
5 The Road to Jerusalem   122
6 The Way to the Cross   150
7 Passion and Resurrection   161

   Notes to Part One   181
   Index of Gospel Sources   183

Part One

LOOKING AT JESUS FROM THE OUTSIDE

Imagine yourself, somewhere around 30 CE, happening upon Jesus near the Sea of Galilee. Perhaps Jesus is out thinking or praying, or just relaxing with his disciples after a day of ministry. Imagine watching him in action or seeing what he looks like. Then imagine sitting down that evening and dashing off a 'letter from the field' to family or friends, or even perhaps to *The Roman Daily Times*, to set the record straight for all open-minded persons. Imagine also trying to describe him as much as possible in non-Christian or even non-religious terms, but without being either irreverent (unless you think appropriate) or disrespectful of those who differ from you.

That is what I shall attempt to do in Chapter 4 below – to draw from the Gospels a picture of Jesus that an imaginary first-century observer would recognize. But first, if I am to draw on the Gospels in this way, we need to consider the question of whether these texts – the sacred scriptures for Christians and the Church for nearly two thousand years – record reliable information.

1 | WHAT ARE THE GOSPELS, AND WHERE DID THEY COME FROM?

Two issues complicate the matter from the start: on the one hand, modern historians have extremely high standards for what can be considered 'proven' and, on the other hand, the first Christians did not operate with or care about such standards of 'proof'. Some simply don't care if the Gospels are reliable, while others tend to make 'proofs' a test of what ought to be believed or not.

So, how did we get the Gospels and was the process secure enough to provide us with reliable information about Jesus? It is best to answer this by first providing a good example of the sort of information we have in the Gospels. But, before we give that example, we need to observe that there are two sorts of 'gospels' in the Christian scriptures.

The first three Gospels are very similar, so similar that they are called the 'synoptic' Gospels. Here 'synoptic' means that the three can be set out in columns and easily compared because each records much of what the others also record. Thus, the Gospels of Matthew, Mark and Luke are the 'synoptic' Gospels and each of them (say, Mark) has much of what is in the others (Matthew and Luke). The fourth Gospel, the Gospel of John, is distinct both in style and in content. If the 'synoptics' tell us about 'kingdom of God' and 'parables' and have a Jesus who does 'miracles', the Gospel of John tells us about 'eternal life' and Jesus speaks in long, winding discourses that revolve around special terms, and this Jesus does 'signs'.

Here's an example of the sort of 'history' we find in the Gospels: when Jesus asks Peter 'Who do you think I am?', Peter's response in the Gospels is as follows:

Matthew: 'You are the Messiah, the Son of the Living God.'
Mark: 'You are the Messiah.'
Luke: 'You are the Messiah of God.'
John: 'You are the Holy One of God.'

And here I am fudging, because the context in John for Peter's so-called 'confession' is considerably different. But regardless of what one does with John, the synoptic Gospels vary. Some people have attempted to 'harmonize' the accounts, and suggest that Peter actually said, 'You are the Messiah, the Son of the Living God, in fact, the Holy One of God.' Others find such explanations unnecessary and merely allow for a 'degree of interpretation' in all records of history and find such paraphrasings and approximations entirely acceptable for what counts as evidence and proof about what Peter (or Jesus) said. This passage illustrates the sort of thing we find every time we read the Gospels.

To understand how we got from Jesus to the Gospels, we must understand that Galilean Judaism was predominantly an *oral* culture and not a *written* culture like ours. A story is told of a certain Rabbi Meir who, when he got to Susa in Babylonia, was informed that they did not have a copy of the book of Esther so he sat down and wrote one out for them. And such a capacity was not seen as extraordinary.

In oral cultures, events are watched and speeches and sayings are heard, and the ordinary person then begins to make sense of it by reciting it or by repeating it, and when he or she gets together with others, they work on a given 'rendition' of that event or speech or story. And, it needs to be observed, oral cultures both remember well and extemporarize effectively in order to make a specific 'performance' effective. They see and they hear and they remember, and what they focus on are the 'big facts' and the 'major sayings' and the 'big picture'. But, when they come to reciting whatever they choose to recite, their given performance will 'colour the situation' or 'set the context' and these colourings and shadings will either be typical or specific, but no one would worry about whether or not the contextual shadings are precisely what was done on that specific occasion.

A good example of what may be called a 'typical' setting can be found in Luke 15 (p. 129) when the parables of the lost sheep, the lost coin and the lost (or prodigal) son are given this setting:

> Another time, the tax-collectors and sinners were all crowding in to listen to him; and the Pharisees and scribes began murmuring their disapproval: 'This fellow', they said, 'welcomes sinners and eats with them.'

Perhaps this is precisely the context for Jesus, and he sat down right then and told each of these three parables in that order. Or, what is more likely for an oral cultural context, Jesus did tell these three stories in roughly this form, and he did tell such stories to a variety of crowds, and he had as one of his target audiences the 'Pharisees and scribes' because it was they who (it was perceived) created the problems by dividing the Land in half at the table.

What we have then in the Gospels is not simply a 'red-letter' *verbatim* quotation of exactly what Jesus said and where he said it and to whom he said it, but instead a reliable oral tradition about what Jesus said and to whom he said such things and where he said such things. If this is the case, we need to remind ourselves that the 'red letter' editions of the Gospels create a modern perception: they lead us to think we have 'explicit and *verbatim* quotations' when we don't really have that (though sometimes we surely do).

Now the thicket gets thicker: not only are the Gospels the result of an oral transmission process, but they are in a language other than what Jesus typically spoke. Scholars who are trained to detect original languages are divided today about what language Jesus most often spoke in. But, most would agree that Jesus spoke in Aramaic or (less likely) in Hebrew or (and this would have been necessarily rare) in Greek or Latin. If Jesus spoke most of his sayings in Aramaic (a dialect of Hebrew) and our Gospels are in

Greek (in the earliest versions we have of them), then not only did the oral process shape the sayings and events, but also the translation process would also have shaped the sayings. For, as anyone who knows a foreign language will admit, it is rare for one language to be translated into another without alterations and adjustments needed to make the most sense.

So, our Gospels are the result of an oral and translation process. At some point along the line from Jesus to the Gospels the oral tradition was suddenly 'frozen' into a 'written form'. When that occurred, the specific saying or event ceased being a 'performance' adjusted by particular contexts and became a 'fixed' tradition. This is not to say that the specific event or saying did not go on being 're-performed' by followers of Jesus for new audiences – for they almost certainly did. One Christian of the second century AD stated that he still preferred the 'living tradition' (oral tradition) over the 'written'. But, the tradition that we now find in the Gospels is the result of an oral tradition that became 'fixed' when it was recorded in our Gospels.

But, even this process is not as simplistic as all that. For it is a matter (as we say) of 'public record' to observe that the individual Evangelists (the authors of our Gospels) also shaped the oral traditions they had in front of them by the way they set them in contexts and by the way they chose to write them out. When we compare the differences in the Evangelists' accounts we can see how they set the record straight for themselves and for the audience or community for whom they wrote their Gospels. For instance, in Matthew (chapter 5) we read, 'Blessed are the poor *in spirit*' whereas in Luke (chapter 6) we read, 'Blessed are the poor.' Again, in Matthew (chapter 5) we read, 'Blessed are those who hunger *and thirst to see right prevail*' whereas in Luke (chapter 6) we read, 'Blessed are those who hunger *now*.' Another example of differences between the synoptic Gospels is with the prayer that in Christian tradition has become known as the 'Our Father' or 'The Lord's Prayer'. We can see the differences clearly if we lay the two renditions side by side:

Matthew's rendition	*Luke's rendition*
Our Father *in heaven*	Father
May your name be hallowed	May your name be hallowed
Your kingdom come	Your kingdom come
Your will be done on earth as it is in heaven	
Give us today our daily bread	Give us today our daily bread
Forgive us the wrong we have done	Forgive us the wrong we have done
As we have forgiven those who have wronged us	For we ourselves forgive everyone who owes us
And do not put us to the test	And do not put us to the test
But save us from the evil one.	

We could go on to give a multitude of examples, but the kinds of differences are clear from what is in italics above: we have explanatory additions, we have adjustments, we have added lines and subtracted words. These changes, if we are comfortable with an oral culture, can be explained by the sorts of things 'oral storytellers' do when they give a 'new performance'. Or, because we are now examining the specifics of an Evangelist's own 'performance', we can begin to ask if these kinds of changes are part and parcel of the way a particular Evangelist writes. We can ask these kinds of questions: Is it the case that Matthew is more concerned with 'spiritual' poverty or is it the case that Luke is concerned with 'material' poverty? Is Matthew concerned with 'justice' (as is clear in the 'to see the right prevail') or is Luke concerned with those who are hungering 'now'? Has Matthew or someone else, perhaps even Jesus on another occasion, added to the 'Our Father' or has Luke 'omitted' things from the same prayer? Do these sorts of changes reflect the specific interests and themes of these Evangelists?

The 'Gospel' that we have in front of us in *The Story of the Christ* is an amalgamation of the four Gospels, which are themselves the result of both an oral process and an editorial process, the result of both storytellers 'performing' the words and events of Jesus, and the Evangelists 'freezing' those performances once and for all. Since oral cultures are good at remembering, and since they have every reason to remember what was most important – after all, they believed 'in' these things about Jesus – we can be assured that what we have in the Gospels is a reliable record of what Jesus said and did, but we cannot expect these things to be *verbatim* reports of everything Jesus said, and to whom and where.

As stated above, there are four Gospels. Three of these are called the 'synoptics' and these three – Matthew, Mark, and Luke – are so interrelated we have what is often called the 'synoptic problem'. Put simply the problem is, what is the relationship of Matthew to Mark and to Luke in all directions? There are several different theories about this.

The first is the 'Oxford Hypothesis', called such because it was largely hammered out at Oxford in the 1900s. It is argued that to begin with, the oral traditions were sporadically 'frozen' into various written traditions, and there are various written traditions behind our synoptic Gospels. It goes like this: first, there were oral traditions; second, someone gathered together the sayings of Jesus into a document that we now call 'Q' (from the German word for 'source', *Quelle*). Third, Mark wrote his Gospel but did not know or use Q. Fourth, various others were putting together traditions about Jesus, and Matthew and Luke each had some access to these. So, fifth, Matthew wrote his Gospel and he did so by 'using' Q, Mark, and an independent tradition now labelled for convenience 'M'. Sixth, Luke wrote his Gospel using Q, Mark, and his own independent tradition called 'L'. For those who agree with this 'Oxford Hypothesis' the process of writing down these traditions begins in the fourth or fifth decade of the first century and ends anywhere from the destruction of Jerusalem until the ninth decade.

The second theory, the 'Griesbach Hypothesis', sees things differently. For scholars who believe in this theory, Matthew first wrote his Gospel; then Luke used Matthew and rearranged much of what Matthew had done and added his own bits of tradition; and then, last, Mark set down to condense or abbreviate what Matthew and Luke had written.

For nearly a century the vast majority of scholars believed the Oxford Hypothesis, but recently there has been a small revival of interest in the older Griesbach Hypothesis. There are advantages and disadvantages with each theory, but one thing is clear: anyone who sits down with separate columns of Gospel sayings and events will observe that there are at times staggering similarities (*verbatim* similarities) and at other times notable dissimilarities. The issues are puzzling enough for this to be called the 'synoptic problem'.

Something should be said about the merits of each hypothesis. The advantage of the Griesbach hypothesis is that it doesn't resort to any 'hypothetical' sources. On the other hand, it is bedevilled by two problems. The first is that it is hard to explain why there needs to be a 'Mark' if Mark is only condensing what is already done (quite well, thank you) in Matthew or Luke. The second problem for the Griesbach proponents, which is actually the strength of the Oxford Hypothesis, is this: if one studies line after line in the synoptic Gospels and asks one question, the result is nearly uniformly in one direction: toward the Oxford Hypothesis. That question is this: given the normal rules of textual criticism for determining such things, which reading most likely gave rise to the other? In other words, if we ask this question of the examples above, and ask 'Is it more likely that Matthew added "in spirit" or that Luke omitted "in spirit"' then the normal rules of evidence, which favour a shorter or simpler reading giving rise to a longer or more complex reading, then it favours that Matthew is secondary to Luke. And, when one does this for the entire synoptic Gospels, the majority of scholars have come to the conclusion that Mark is the most original

Gospel, and that both Matthew and Luke used Mark when they wrote their Gospels.

Because of the sheer complexity of specific examples and the inability of scholars studying the matter to come to a consensus, a number of scholars today have opted out of this discussion and have appealed to a third theory: that in fact the synoptic Gospels are independent of one another at the written level but that they are each dependent on similar 'oral' traditions. This oral tradition was used independently by Matthew, by Mark, and by Luke, and each of these writers is independent of the others. The matter is not as simple as this, and there remain problems even for this 'opt-out' approach, but there are advantages, not the least of which is that the early Christians lived and breathed an oral culture. If scholars can one day find a solution to the 'synoptic problem' it may well help in clarifying the development of earliest Christianity.

The long and short of this matter is clear: the Gospels we now have are the result of both oral and written processes, but with a growing awareness of scholarship today that the oral process was first and had a decisive impact on both the reliability and the shaping of the Gospels that we now read. There is a general consensus – with voices against in both directions – that the Gospels are generally reliable, but that we should avoid the impression that our Gospels are *verbatim* reports of what Jesus said and did. Both the oral storytellers and the Evangelists themselves had a 'hand' in the shaping of the Gospels, and those hands shaped the Gospels in the direction of concerns and issues of their own day.

Because *The Story of the Christ* puts together only the four Gospels of the traditional Christian canon (the books accepted as authoritative by the early Church), there is very little reason here to engage in debate about those gospels that the early Church did not include in the canon. Some of these non-canonical gospels have been given much attention, like 'The Gospel of Thomas', but no one contends that these other gospels were more original at each and every point. Instead, what most today are arguing for is that the early Christians who 'silenced' the voices of alternative gospels need themselves to be silenced, and that the alternative voices of the first four centuries of the Church need to be given a fair hearing in a new generation, in which some no longer accept the early Christian judgements about which Gospels to include and which Gospels to exclude in the canon for Christians. However, it remains a fact that the Four Gospels of the Christian canon have shaped the entire history of the Church and have shaped 'the story of the Christ' to such a degree that any turning back either to rewrite history or the 'story' of the Christ is both unlikely and more than a little problematic even for those who would like a chance at it.

2 | WHAT WAS RELIGION LIKE AT THE TIME OF JESUS?

Jesus' contemporaries, because of a long history of misunderstanding and abuse, deserve to be given a fresh hearing. Jews at the time of Jesus were not all alike, they were not all obsessed with the *Torah*, they did not run around like the American Puritan Jonathan Edwards' father, Timothy Edwards, railing on the local youth who used foul language and told bawdy stories and did too much night-walking. Because of Western Christian stereotypes, the first thing readers of the Gospels need to learn is that Jesus' opponents were normal human beings who were also trying to live before God responsibly. Husbands and wives loved one another and they loved their children; they were good neighbours; there were decent folk. Knowing they had a special history and living out their lives with respect to the *Torah* may at times have separated some Jews (not all) from the ordinary Gentile, but this was done only because they thought their *Torah* prescribed such boundary-making.

Israel's Story and its Markers

In essence, all Jews were identified by four markers: they had an ethnic identity, they lived in a Land they believed was given them by God, they followed the *Torah* (more or less), and the centre of their faith and society was the Temple in Jerusalem. These four 'markers' of Judaism were learned and made known to future generations in the shape of a 'story'. The Gospels give us Jesus' own interpretation of this story.

For Jews at the time of Jesus and beyond, the story of Judaism contains the following elements:

1. God, known to Jews by the name *YHWH*, is the Creator God.
2. God creates Adam and Eve, and they are specifically designed by God to be his very own 'images', or (to transliterate the Greek translation of the Hebrew Bible) his very own *Eikons*. Adam and Eve are God's *Eikons* designed to reflect the glory of God, but instead of reflecting that glory, they choose their own way and sin (Genesis 1—3).
3. Because of sin, they are saddled with selfishness and the world begins to unravel through murder, isolation from one another, and the rebellious sabotaging of the *Eikons* God made when humans decide to make their own *eikons* (carved images) of what they think God is like. But, God does not abandon his special *Eikons*.
4. To restore Adam's and Eve's descendants to their *Eikonic* glory, God forms a 'covenant' with Abraham and then later with Moses and then even later with David – and he gives Israel the Land, and he gives them a Temple, and he makes them a nation.
5. The promise inherent to these various chapters in Israel's story is that *YHWH* will be Israel's God but Israel must make *YHWH* its sole God to whom Israel is to be faithful. If Israel is faithful, God will 'bless' Israel and her Land and her Temple.
6. But Israel (as the story unfolds) is not faithful, and so Israel wakes up one morning in a foreign country, or as the biblical 'storytellers' say it, in 'exile', only to be promised once again (in God's grace) that
7. if Israel 'repents', God will restore Israel once again to the Land.

Hence, the subsequent 'chapters' shape this foundational 'story' for all of Israel: God as creator, humans as cracked *Eikons*, God's election of Israel to bless her, Israel's wanderings in and out of that blessing of God, God's endless graciousness. This story gives particular shape to the previously noted four 'markers' of Israel – ethnic identity, Land, *Torah* and Temple.

One's *ethnic identity* may be disputable, but one's status following proper investigation can usually be settled. If your mother was Jewish, you were Jewish; if your father was Jewish, you might be Jewish. In disputed cases, guidelines were established. A good example, known to readers of the New Testament, is the case of Timothy, a travel companion of the Apostle Paul (Acts 16:1–5). Timothy's mother was Jewish (and a believer in Jesus as Messiah) but his father was a Greek (and perhaps not a believer). To 'clarify' Timothy's status, Paul had him circumcised. (Circumcision, which today is little more than a health measure in most Western countries, was established with Abraham (Genesis 17) as a visible male marker of those who belonged to Israel. Refusal to circumcize was a form of apostasy.) Now Timothy was a Jew because his mother was Jewish, but his father was Greek (a Gentile) and he was uncircumcized. Circumcision made his status clear (for those who cared to look when they were at the gymnasium). If you are asking, what you may have heard is probably accurate: female 'status' was established by the male to whom they were connected through marriage or parentage. Because circumcision was painful, it was easier for females to convert to Judaism than for males and, because Christianity did not settle into the circumcision requirement for Gentile converts, conversion to Christianity was easier for males. So, one of the markers for Judaism was ethnic identity, largely embodied by the act of circumcision.

The *Land* of Israel, a promise granted to Abraham in ages past, became a central feature of Israelite faith: to dwell in the Land meant to enjoy God's blessings and approval; to dwell outside the Land (in the Diaspora) meant to experience the displeasure of God. If the Land promise comes to Israel through Abraham, the *Torah* comes to Israel at the hand of Moses. The *Torah* is a Hebrew term for 'instruction', hence the term in the Bible can refer to any particular law (also called a *mitzvah*, hence a *bar mitzvah* is a 'son of the law') or to a specific body of 'laws' (like Deuteronomy) or to a collection of books (like the Pentateuch, the first five books of the Old Testament; or, as is sometimes the case, to the entire collection of books now called the 'Old' Testament by Christians or the 'Hebrew Bible' by Jews). It needs to be observed that for Jews, contrary to what those who have been reared in the Christian faith in the tradition of the Reformation have been taught, the *Torah* was a gift from God to his people so they would know how best to live. To be Jewish, to live in the Land, and to obey the *Torah* was what it meant to be quintessentially Jewish and to live under the blessing of God.

The 'Land' promise of Genesis 12 is ultimately narrowed down to one specific plot of land: the Temple. The Temple had its precursor in the 'mobile tent' of ancient Israelites as they wandered through the wilderness from Egypt to the Promised Land, but under Solomon the Temple was finally built and it became the centre of a 'Temple-nation state' from that time on (well, roughly). God filled the Temple with his presence and he promised his presence whenever Israel lived faithfully. When Israel was 'deported' to Babylonia (in the sixth century BCE), the Temple fell into ruins, but when Israel returned, the leaders of Israel (Ezra, Nehemiah) enabled Israel to rebuild the walls, and the Temple and the Land was (in part) restored to them.

But, because there were disputes about each of these four markers of Jewish belief and practice, which led to various 'stories' for Israel, Judaism was diverse. Some today prefer even to speak of 'Judaisms' rather than 'Judaism'. As evidence for diversity within Judaism at the time of Jesus, there are the four major 'parties' or 'denominations' known as Sadducees, Pharisees, Zealots and Essenes. What distinguishes each is not a 'creed' so much as a 'way of living' the *Torah*. The centre of the various Judaisms then was not ortho*doxy* (right belief) but ortho*praxy* (right practice), and as such need to be carefully distinguished from current Christian denominations (where theological tenets form dividing lines).

Because the Pharisees are so central to the Gospels, a brief word can be given about the other three before we turn to the Pharisees.

Sadducees, Zealots, Essenes

The *Sadducees* were the landed aristocrats of the Land of Israel: they were the priests and they ran the Temple. Because they were the aristocrats in 'power' at the time the Temple was destroyed by Titus of Rome (*c.* 70 CE) and because those who gained 'power' after that time were wary of connection with the Sadducees, the Sadducees virtually disappeared from history after the Temple's destruction. It is likely, because he was a priest, that the father of John the Baptist, Zechariah, was a Sadducee or at least sympathetic with their concerns – which was the maintenance of the Temple and its system. They were less 'liberal' than the typical Pharisee, which is to say they were politically and religiously 'conservative'. (I use the terms 'liberal' and 'conservative' because it helps us see the 'Pharisees' in their socio-political context, even if one needs to be careful of imposing our social agendas on ancient groups.)

Josephus, a Jewish historian of the first century, claims that the Sadducees were boorish and believed only in the first five books of Moses (Genesis, Exodus, Leviticus, Numbers, Deuteronomy) and that they did not believe in the 'resurrection' of the dead. When he attempts to provide an analogy of what Sadducees think to his largely Roman audience, Josephus says the Sadducees 'do away with Fate (*heimarmene*) altogether, and remove God beyond . . . the very sight of evil . . . they maintain that man has the free choice of good or evil'.[1]

The influence of the Sadducees was enormous, but limited largely to what took place in Jerusalem during the High Holidays. We do not know what percentage of Jews attended the major feasts (Rosh Hashanah, Yom Kippur, though the specifically pilgrim festivals are Passover [*Pesah*], Weeks [*Shavuot*], and Booths [*Sukkot*]). A good guess is that each family attended one of these festivals per year. The holidays were family events, full of food (even some red meat) and fun and fellowship (like contemporary Jewish and Christian and Muslim religious holidays), and we can surmise that many Jews attended, perhaps even into the hundreds of thousands. Most of the time, the calendar, the events and the liturgical matters were established and administered by the Sadducees. Disputes between groups, even between leaders, revved up the crowds at times.

Behind the Sadducees were the Romans, and the Sadducees found themselves as leaders of Jerusalem and of a nation in need of careful co-operation with Rome. During the lifetime of Jesus, the Roman Emperors were Augustus (Octavian) and Tiberius; the Roman appointed leaders included Herod the Great (*d.* 4 BC) and Herod Antipas, as well as the procurator Pontius Pilate (26–36 CE).

If the Sadducees co-operated with Rome, another party found Rome insufferable. The Zealots, known more for their attitude toward Rome and their violence than for anything else, describes a party that some think existed even at the time of Jesus, though many today conclude that this party had its specific origins in events and persons more toward the middle of the first century CE. At any rate, we know about them mostly through Josephus, and he chooses to make them the 'scapegoat' for the war with Rome that brought Jerusalem to its knees. What we do know about the Zealots is that they were a militaristically inclined sect of Judaism. Whether the party existed or not at the time of Jesus is of less concern than that the 'spirit' of zealotry – violence is compatible with the work of God and can be used to establish the will of God – was part and parcel of first-century Judaism. That one of Jesus' own followers was called a 'Zealot' means probably just that – although he may well have abandoned such a *modus operandi* to follow Jesus.

The Essenes are a story in and of themselves. In 1947 a Bedouin tossed a rock into the opening of a cave near the village of Khirbet Qumran, heard something break, entered the cave, and the discovery of the Dead Sea Scrolls began – but not without plenty of plot and politics. While some suggest that the 'Essenes' are not identical with the community at Qumran, the general consensus today is that they are or are very close to identical.

The Essenes were a sect of Judaism that broke with the ruling establishment (probably Sadducees or Pharisees) in Jerusalem, moved themselves out of the holy city and established their headquarters along the Dead Sea near Khirbet Qumran. They show all the signs of normal religious sectarian radical groups: too many rigorous rules that separate them both from other Jews and from one another if need be, too rigid of hierarchical authority, and too much vindictiveness with respect to others with similar, but not identical enough, beliefs and practices. What stands out today are their distinctive way of reading the *Torah*, which always spoke about them and the times in which they were living, their conviction that God was on their side and that the 'holy war' that was imminent would vindicate them, and their assortment of liturgical and communal practices.

Before we get to the Pharisees, we should observe that most Jews were not aligned with one of these parties, and that most Jews would have sympathized at times with various features of each of these groups. Jews of the Land of Israel can be distinguished from Jews of the Diaspora. The latter are Jews who lived outside the Land, and who were more or less assimilated into the surrounding culture. However, lines were clearly drawn on matters sacred to Judaism – like the belief in one God (monotheism), the sacredness of their laws and their ethnic identity and their Temple. Not all Jews in the Land of Israel were Pharisees; not all followed the *Torah* with rigour; and not all were worried too much about the Romans. Some Jews, later dubbed the *Am ha-aretz* ('people of the Land'), had little concern or time to worry about *Torah* regulations, but most probably did. The Roman presence in the Land of Israel, with a military post just a few miles north of Nazareth in a village called Sepphoris, was of more concern to some than to others. Jesus says very little about the Romans, and this may well indicate that Rome was more tolerated than despised.

Pharisees

Pharisees are often depicted by Christians as Dante depicted a certain Fra Gomita of Gallura, as 'a vessel fit for every fraud'.[2] While this may be true of the Fra Gomita who took bribes, this is not true about Pharisees – who, in most cases, were God-fearing, *Torah*-observing, nation-loving Jews. Some think of the Pharisees the way we may think of Dimsdale, Hawthorne's stereotyped but disgusting pastor in *The Scarlet Letter* who had his way with Hester Prinn and hoped others would not have their way with him. We know these Pharisee stereotypes, but we should not equate them with Pharisees. In fact, it is unfortunate (for the Pharisees and for our perception of them) that the term 'pharisaical' means what it does.

But it was the Pharisees who most often went toe-to-toe with Jesus and, because the story is usually told by Christians, their reputation got stuck in reverse. Each of the two, the Pharisees and Jesus, lost confidence in each other as a result of their constant toe-tapping over what God expected of his people – with Jesus saying one thing and the Pharisees saying something else. Pharisees might best be seen as persons thoroughly committed to the *Torah* and its obedience. Because of their commitment, they were just as committed to 'interpreting' that *Torah* in such a manner that it could be reasonably practised by all who cared to follow its directives. In particular, they seem to be most concerned with food laws (eating only *kosher* food), in addition to having more than a little interest in such matters as Sabbath practice. Pharisees apparently may have (not all would agree) eaten normal meals the way priests ate meals in the Temple, and this seems to be a defining practice of the Pharisees.[3]

The foundation for their beliefs and practices, as has been mentioned, was the *Torah*, especially texts like Leviticus and Deuteronomy. But, in addition, the Pharisees distinguished themselves from the Sadducees because they believed in the authority of the entire *Tanakh* (The *Torah*, the *Neviim*, and the *Ketuvim*, the Law, the Prophets, and the Writings). And, this

Tanakh was supplemented and interpreted in a living way by orally passing on traditional interpretations by authoritative teachers. Now, just how much of this was going on, not even to mention specifically what *content* was being passed on at the time of Jesus, is no longer possible to tell. But, when we see in Mark 7 or Matthew 23 the disputes Jesus is having with Pharisees and scribes over specific interpretations and oral traditions, we can be sure that we are staring at the sort of thing Jesus and the Pharisees often did.

There is only one really substantial text from an outsider who comments on Jesus. His name is Josephus, though the text in question has probably been tampered with by Christians, who are the preservers of Josephus' many works. Here is what the text now says:

> About this time comes Jesus, a wise man [if indeed it is proper to call him a man]. For he was a worker of incredible deeds, a teacher of those who accept the truth with pleasure, and he attracted many Jews as well as Greeks. [This man was Messiah.] And when, in view of his denunciation by the leading men among us, Pilate had him sentenced to a cross, those who had loved him at the beginning did not cease. [He appeared to them on the third day alive again, for the divine prophets had announced these and countless other marvels concerning him.] And even now the tribe of the 'Christians' – named after him – has not yet disappeared.

The bracketed words are what most think are clear 'Christian interpolations' but most today think Josephus did say something about Jesus and that it was mostly positive, if also disinterested.

Which leads us back to the Gospels' portrait of the Pharisees (and other Jewish groups) and to our characterization of what Jesus was like to the outsider. When we read what the Gospels say about the various Jewish groups with whom Jesus was in conflict, we need to be aware that the language of those debates is written from a Christian perspective. Hence, we need to avoid identifying polemical description with routine normalities. I do not dispute that some Pharisees were fastidious in their observance and at times an annoyance to others, but that reality should not lead the modern interpreter to think all Pharisees were always like this or (and this is worse) that all modern Jews are like fastidious Pharisees. It must at least be appreciated that fastidiousness in *Torah* observance is understood by most of its practitioners as an opportunity to do God's will. Jesus disagreed not about the importance of radical obedience, but about what God's will really was.

3 | WHAT WERE THE MAIN THEMES OF JESUS' TEACHING?

Neither Jews of the time nor Jesus learn 'theology' by studying it philosophically or by proving it in the context of academic debate or by 'going to university or seminary'. Instead, in the same way that modern children learn to value freedom and human rights, so Jesus 'imbibes' Judaism from his father and his mother and his extended family and his community. And the first thing he learns comes to him in the form of a sacred creed that is known as much by living it out as by thinking one's way through it. 'Theology' is more caught than taught, and what is caught is a variation on the old four-marker theme: ethnic identity, Land, *Torah* and Temple. That story is a theology, and that theology is caught in the web of daily recitation of a creed.

Shema

As a young child, Jesus would have been taught by his father and his mother to begin and end his day by reciting (aloud) the sacred *Shema*:

> Hear, Israel: the Lord is our God, the Lord our one God; and you must love the Lord your God with all your heart and with all your soul and with all your strength.
>
> These commandments which I give you this day are to be remembered and taken to heart; repeat them to your children, and speak of them both indoors and out of doors, when you lie down and when you get up. Bind them as a sign on your hand and wear them as a pendant on your forehead; write them on the doorposts of your houses and on your gates.

Here is the shape of Israel's 'theology': there is only one God; his name is *YHWH*; Israel is to love him with every globule of its being – heart, soul and strength. And, to keep this fundamental relationship to the one God intact, Israel is to remind itself constantly of its centrality.[4]

How? They are to memorize the *Shema* themselves; they are to educate their children through the *Shema*; they are to say the *Shema* when they leave the home and when they enter the home; they are to recite the *Shema* when they retire at night and when they arise in the morning; they are to write the *Shema* on a parchment, place it in a small container, and strap it to their head and to their arm (a *phylactery*) and wear it, the way Franciscans wear a brown habit; and they are to attach the *Shema*, again in a small container, to doorposts and to gates (a *mezuzah*) right where most today have their house numbers. Some understood these commandments more literally than others, but the point remains the same: loving God by following his *Torah* was to order the life of the ordinary Israelite and to give that life a story and a 'theology'.

God as Father
Jesus learns about God and about Israel and about his own relationship to God and Israel through the *Shema*, and the key word in that *Shema* is to 'love' God. And, like any teacher of his day, Jesus carries on this tradition about God and develops it in his own way. *God*, whose personal name is *YHWH* for Jews, Jesus most often calls *Abba*, which is the Aramaic word for 'father'. Some scholarship overcooks the meaning of *Abba* for Jesus, suggesting that Jesus means 'daddy' in the sense of a childlike address to God or that his understanding of God in terms of *Abba* far transcends in intimacy anything ever seen in Judaism. Namely, that Jesus sees God in more personal and immanent terms than had ever been seen in Judaism. Both of these notions are overdone. It is historically accurate to say of Jesus that *Abba* is his distinctive emphasis – for him, God is to be called and to be related to as *Abba*. And this is the language of the home and the

family and the language of love and trust. But, Israel had a long history of calling God *Abba*, not the least of which passages would be Hosea 11:1–4:

> When Israel was a youth, I loved him;
> out of Egypt I called my son;
> but the more I called, the farther they went from me;
> they must needs sacrifice to the baalim and burn offerings
> to images.
> It was I who taught Ephraim to walk,
> I took them in my arms;
> but they did not know that I secured them with reins
> and led them with bonds of love,
> that I lifted them like a little child to my cheek,
> that I bent down to feed them.

Regardless of what Jesus means by calling God *Abba*, there is nothing more expressive of God's tender and familial love in the Bible than this passage. Hosea 11:1–4, in fact, can be seen as a commentary on what *Abba*'s love for his people is like according to Jesus, and it is perhaps one of the places Jesus learned what God's love was like. So, the term *Abba* is thoroughly Jewish, even if Jesus emphasizes it more than any teacher in ancient Israel. Furthermore, the term *Abba*, while it is familial, is not 'childlike'. The term *Abba*, or its Hebrew counterpart, *Av*, is both the first term a child learns for his or her father and it remains the only term that child has for his or her father as long as the child is alive.

That Jesus emphasizes that God is one who loves humans is beyond question, but this love of God for humans and the corresponding love of humans for God is at the same time *sacred* or 'holy'. The term 'holy' (from the Hebrew *qodesh*) has two important elements: 'holy' refers to the utter difference between God and humans/the created world, and 'holy' refers to God's moral impeccability. A fundamental idea in the Old Testament is that God is 'holy' in these two senses: he is vast, immense, omnipresent and omniscient and unlike anything else known on planet earth; and he always does what is good and right and best. And, since God is like this, God's relations to his created world and the created world's relation to God reflect that 'holiness'.

It is unfortunate that the term 'holiness', especially when set in a religious context today, evokes the fastidiousness of the Puritans or the isolation of the contemplative or the squeamishness of the sectarian or the zealotry of the radicals rather than what is the norm of any genuinely loving relationship. As love for one's spouse or children is 'holy' in that we don't give that love to anyone else, so love for God is to be 'holy' in that Israel doesn't give that love to any other god.

Because God is loving and because God's love is sacred (or 'holy'), the relationship of an Israelite to God is also to be 'holy' or 'sacred'. Thus, from Leviticus 19:2: 'You must be holy, because I, the Lord your God, am holy.' This draws us back to the former line of thinking: the story of Israel is shaped by a covenant, and that covenant is that God will be Israel's God if Israel will let God be their God. And, if God's love for Israel is 'holy', then Israel is to maintain its love for God in loyalty, fidelity and sanctity. If God's love for Israel is 'holy', then Israel's corresponding love is also to be 'holy'. Which means, one cannot love God and love other gods at the same time. 'Idolatry' is condemned in the Bible because it violates Israel's sacred love for God. The prophet Hosea, especially in chapters 1—2, spells out Israel's relationship to *YHWH* in these very terms: acts of disobedience to the covenant are like heinous infidelities to a spouse!

This holy love for God creates 'reverence' in one's approach to God. Not only is Israel to be holy, but Israel is also to speak of God in a holy manner. Readers of the Bible will observe that in most English translations the word 'Lord' is sometimes rendered 'LORD'. There is a reason for this. In the Hebrew Bible, or what Christians call the Old Testament, there are three major words used when referring to God: first, there is *El* or its plural form *Elohim* and it is translated as 'God'; then there is *Adonai* and it is translated as 'Lord'; but, the personal name for God in the Bible is *YHWH* and it is normally translated as 'LORD'. So, when an English reader sees this spelling, the reader is invited to understand the sacred name of God. Furthermore, because Israel was told in the Ten Commandments not to take the 'name' of God 'in vain', it became customary well before the first Century CE to obey that commandment by 'evasion'. That is, instead of saying the sacred name *YHWH* and risking using it 'in vain', it became the custom not to say that name and instead to substitute *Adonai* in its place. What strikes modern readers as a little 'over the top' was for the Jew an expression of 'holy' devotion. Jesus was very much like his contemporaries in this regard, and it is expressed in what has become the most memorable thing Jesus ever said – the 'Our Father' or the 'Lord's Prayer'. In this prayer Jesus carries on the typical Jewish reverence for God's sacred name: '. . . may your name [*YHWH*] be hallowed' (p. 97). It was also customary for Jews of Jesus' day to refer to God as *Ha-Shem* ('the Name').

That God was holy did not make God so transcendent that Jews were somehow afraid of God; no, God's covenant loving kindness was a fixture of a Jewish understanding of God. And, because God is loving in such a manner, Jesus teaches his followers to trust and love God in return; because God is holy, Jesus teaches his followers to be holy and to be righteous and to be fully committed to God. Loving God and living before him in fidelity is what the covenant is all about. Jesus believes that Israel's present condition – in subordination to Rome, morals less than what they should be, parties arguing with another, Jerusalem's leadership in league with Rome and abusing its power, the number of Israelites marginalized by poverty – these conditions and others are a stark reminder that Israel's 'exile' is really not over. For Israel to experience the blessing of God, and for the kingdom of God to become a reality in the Land of Israel, Israel must turn from its ways, tell the truth about its sinfulness to *YHWH*, and turn back to loving God and to loving others as *YHWH* has said.

When it does, but only *if* it does, God's kingdom can come.

God's Kingdom

The first word Mark records Jesus uttering is about the 'kingdom of God'. He sums up the whole mission of Jesus with these words: 'The time has arrived; the kingdom of God is upon you. Repent, and believe in the gospel' (Mark 1:15). Jesus calls the entire nation to repent in light of the dawning of the kingdom of God. But, any reader of *The Story of the Christ* needs to ask, what is this 'kingdom of God'?

First, we must clarify a terminological issue. Most translations of the Four Gospels use two major expressions for 'kingdom': one is 'kingdom of God' and the other, found especially in Matthew, is 'kingdom of heaven'. (Actually, the Greek behind our translation 'heaven' is plural and could just as easily be translated 'kingdom of heavens'. This is because the Hebrew or Aramaic behind such an expression would also have been plural [e.g., *malkuta shamayim*].) But, the 'kingdom of God' and the 'kingdom of heaven' denote the same in Jesus' world. As it was typical for Jewish piety to use *Adonai*/Lord instead of the sacred name, so it was just as typical for Jewish piety to avoid mentioning 'God': so the kingdom of 'God' was often expressed more reverentially as the kingdom of 'heaven'. What should be observed here is that when 'kingdom of heaven' is used in the Gospels, the meaning of 'heaven' is not 'heaven' as a far-off place in the sky, nor is it a reference in the first instance to 'Eternity' in the proper sense, but instead 'kingdom of heaven' means 'God's kingdom' – and most of the time it is referring to a 'time and space' expression of God's perfect will. The concern with the eternal heaven, which so preoccupied Christian in John Bunyan's timeless classic, *The Pilgrim's Progress*, can be found in other biblical texts, but the 'kingdom of heaven' about which Jesus speaks needs to be dragged down from those lofty heights to make itself visible in the here and now.

Second, 'kingdom' always refers to a 'society' in some sense. So, when Jesus announces that the 'kingdom of God is upon you' he means that God's kingdom, the society in which his will and his people will live in utter *shalom*, is on the verge of arrival. This 'social' dimension of 'kingdom' needs to be kept in mind as one reads through *The Story of the Christ*. Jesus' primary vision for what God is doing through him is shaped by this term 'kingdom'. Many examples could be given, but Jesus' inaugural sermon in his hometown synagogue illustrates this 'social' dimension of kingdom quite effectively. When given the chance to read from the scriptures, Jesus opens the scroll to Isaiah and reads:

> 'The spirit of the Lord is upon me
> because he has anointed [a word connected to *Messiah*] me.'

And observe what the prophet imagines this Spirit-inspired work of the Messiah will be:

> 'he has sent me to announced good news to the poor,
> to proclaim release for prisoners
> and recovery of sight for the blind;
> to let the broken victims go free,
> to proclaim the year of the Lord's favour.' (p. 81)

And once when John the Baptist, who was imprisoned at the time, sent his followers to ask if Jesus was all that the people were saying about him, Jesus said this in response to John, again drawing from the prophet Isaiah:

> 'Go and tell John what you have seen and heard:
> the blind regain their sight,
> the lame walk,
> lepers are made clean,
> the deaf hear,
> the dead are raised to life,
> the poor are brought good news
> and happy is he who does not find me an obstacle to faith.' (p. 104)

By 'kingdom' Jesus envisions a society in which God's healing ways will restore all persons to their proper place (called 'justice' in the Bible), and these persons will be restored in heart, soul, mind and body. The kingdom of which Jesus speaks and for which he longs is a kingdom of *shalom* and justice and love.

It is not that Jesus is an anarchist who thought we ought to return to some supposed 'state of nature' in which all humans could do whatever they wanted. In fact, I suspect Jesus would listen in on the Polish philosopher, Leszek Kolakowski and up him one notch. Kolakowski once said of power:[5]

It is fairly plain, therefore, that if the institutions of political power were miraculously to vanish, the result would not be universal brotherhood but universal slaughter.

This somewhat Hobbesian perception of the 'law of the claw' is not what Jesus envisions in his 'kingdom' but instead Jesus imagines a society in which the good and the powerful are one and the same, in which everyone does what was right, in which everyone would look after his neighbour in the same way he or she looked after one's own interests, and one in which laws would suddenly describe not ideals but realities.

'Kingdom' then is the society in which persons are made whole – in heart, in soul, in mind, and in body. It is populated by those who follow Jesus, who find in him the hope of the ages, and who are healed by him in such a manner that they are 'restored *Eikons*' who now reflect the glory of God by both loving God and loving others completely. No one can accuse Jesus of anything but an ideal, utopian kingdom. When God's kingdom comes, everything will be perfect. His kingdom is the *shalom* everyone dreams of.

In this 'kingdom society' of Jesus *all* persons will be welcome to the 'table of fellowship'. One of the most notable features of Jesus' ministry is that he uses the table to embody his kingdom. So, one of the first events in *The Story of the Christ* is the 'wedding at Cana', at which setting Jesus announces the arrival of the kingdom in the images of 'abundant wine' and 'wedding feasts' (p. 77). When he calls Levi to abandon his toll-collecting to follow him, Jesus immediately shares a meal with him and with his tax-collecting friends – and this act of Jesus draws heavy fire (p. 84–5). Jesus justifies sitting at table with such persons by saying, 'It is not the healthy who need a doctor, but the sick; I did not come to call the virtuous, but sinners.' Over and over, Jesus uses the table as a place where his view of an 'all-inclusive' fellowship can find reality. If his kingdom is utopian, it is not Arcadian, for he expects his view to be 'flesh and blood' at his table. It is easy, one might say, to believe in a kingdom of all sorts until you have to sit down with those sorts.

For Jesus, though, the kingdom is not to be understood as 'glory and might and power and flash and bang', nor does it come with a 'stomp and clap'. Repeatedly, Jesus uses ordinary images, in fact downright humble images, to express his vision of the kingdom. Thus, the kingdom is like the man who plants seeds, goes to sleep and upon waking discovers that the plants are growing. Again, the kingdom is like a 'mustard seed' which, though small and tiny, grows big enough to house birds in its shade. Instead of using the flash and power of military imagery, Jesus uses ordinary images to describe his kingdom: the kingdom is invisible and it begins rather small, but some day, so Jesus is suggesting, it will grow and become a place of refreshment for many.

No one reading *The Story of the Christ* can fail to ask, 'When did Jesus think the kingdom might appear?' That is, did Jesus think the kingdom society was 'imminent' or was it just 'immanent'? The latter spatial term suggests that the 'kingdom' was largely a 'spiritual experience' of the presence and saving activity of God, while the former temporal term suggests that the kingdom was a society that was about to appear miraculously and as a direct act of God. The evidence is divided, and one can be forgiven for thinking now one and now another thing about the 'timing' of the kingdom's arrival. There is, however, no reason to get stuck, like Buridan's ass between two bundles of hay, in deciding which to choose. The evidence suggests one can 'eat from both bundles'.

In Mark 1:15, quoted above, Jesus says, 'the kingdom of God is upon you' and this surely sounds like the kingdom is 'about to arrive'. And several texts suggest that the kingdom is 'imminent'. In Matthew 10:23 (p. 102), Jesus says to the disciples when they are sent out to evangelize the cities of Israel that 'before you have gone through all the towns of Israel the Son of Man will have come'. Just before the so-called 'Transfiguration', an event recorded in the Gospels in which Jesus' very body seems to undergo glorious metamorphosis, Jesus says, 'Truly I tell you: there are some of those standing here who will not taste death before they have seen the Son of Man coming in his kingdom' (p. 117). And, when Jesus predicts the downfall of Jerusalem during his final confrontation with the authorities in Jerusalem, Jesus (after predicting celestial signs) says, 'In the same way, when you see this happening, you may know that the end is near, at the very door. Truly I tell you: the present generation will live to see it all' (p. 158).

On the other hand, there are many more statements of Jesus that suggest that there will be long delay and that the kingdom of God is somehow 'already present' or 'immanent'. Here is an important interaction by Jesus with some of his contemporaries (p. 134):

The Pharisees asked him, 'When will the kingdom of God come?' He answered, 'You cannot tell by observation when the kingdom of God comes. You cannot say, "Look, here it is," or "There it is!" For the kingdom of God is among you!'

This statement suggests that 'kingdom' refers to something 'immanent' in the sense of 'already present' – and therefore more on the level of faith and spiritual presence than 'social revolution'. Another example can be considered: when Jesus is being rigorously queried about exorcising demons, Jesus has just the right response. He says, 'But if it is by the Spirit of God that I drive out the devils, then be sure that the kingdom of God has already come upon you' (p. 106).

Only one reasonable conclusion can be drawn from the evidence we find in the Gospels: Jesus taught that the kingdom was in some sense already immanent and he taught as well that the kingdom (or its final more glorious manifestation) was imminent. The kingdom is present without consummation; it has been inaugurated, he seems to be saying. But, another day is coming.

As a summary and broad definition, I offer this: the 'kingdom' of Jesus is the society in which God's will is done and in which humans are restored to be the sorts of persons God wants them to be and in which humans interact to form the society of *shalom*. The age-old covenant story of Israel is for Jesus a 'kingdom story' in which each of the four markers play their appropriate role: the ethnic identity of Israel is now understood to be inclusive of all; the Land of Israel is what his followers will inherit if they are 'gentle' – here we are suggesting that 'earth' is more expansive in translation than Jesus means when he says 'Blessed are the gentle; they shall have the *earth* for their possession' (p. 93); the *Torah* is given a new shape through the double commandment to love God and others (see below); and the Temple is turned on its head: the place of purity is not the Temple but the heart (p. 93).

How, one is naturally led to ask, does one 'enter the kingdom of God'? There are two answers, and those two answers are two sides of one coin.

Ethics

The simplest way is to state the two answers: one enters the kingdom by 'repentance' and by 'faith'. However, Jesus does not permit his demand to be reduced to a narrow formula for entering the kingdom of God. Instead, as one reads *The Story of the Christ* one will observe that Jesus seems to give a different answer about 'entrance requirements' every time he is asked!

If one is struck by the sheer variety of his responses to those who ask him about entering the kingdom, one is also struck by the bewildering profundity of those same responses, and his responses are radical and challenging and (if one is honest) disturbing to most of his audience at one time or another.

Notice the following statements, and ask yourself the simple question, 'What did Jesus expect of his followers in order for them to enter the kingdom?'

'I tell you, unless you show yourselves far better than the scribes and Pharisees, you can never enter the kingdom of Heaven.' (p. 94)[6]

'Not everyone who says to me, "Lord, Lord" will enter the kingdom of Heaven, but only those who do the will of my heavenly Father.' (p. 99)

'Truly I tell you: unless you turn round and become like children, you will never enter the kingdom of Heaven.' (p. 120)

'Children, how hard it is to enter the kingdom of God! It is easier for a camel to pass through the eye of a needle than for a rich man to enter the kingdom of God.' (p. 136)

Hearing such sayings, we may be tempted to join the closest followers of Jesus in asking Jesus what comes tumbling from their hearts after he makes such statements: 'Then who can be saved?' or 'What should a person do?' In the above sayings, we can say that Jesus seems to expect his followers to be righteous, to do God's will, to be humble, and to abandon riches. But is it *always* necessary to do this? And must one do *all* of this? And what does it mean to *enter* the kingdom?

Repent and believe
We can look at these questions by considering two other words that Jesus uses, 'repent' and 'believe'. In Mark 1:15, Jesus calls his followers to 'repent' and to 'believe'. To 'repent' means to 'turn

from sin and self back to the covenant and to God'. A perfect example of this is found in the self-reflections of the prodigal son who 'discovered himself' while off in a far country doing things contrary to Israel's covenant with God. Luke 15:18–19 (p. 130) reads,

> Then he came to his senses: 'How many of my father's hired servants have more food than they can eat,' he said, 'and here am I, starving to death! I will go at once to my father, and say to him, 'Father, I have sinned against God and against you; I am no longer fit to be called your son; treat me as one of your hired servants.' So he set out for his father's house.

Here is repentance in action: the young man sees his failures to love God and to love his father; he realizes how miserably he has failed both; he confesses his sin to his father; he asks for and trusts in his father's mercy; and (what is most visible) he abandons his former life and returns home. Such a 'repentance' is most welcome to the father of the parable and the God of Jesus.

In addition to 'repentance', Mark 1:15 calls the followers of Jesus to 'believe'. To 'believe' in the kingdom and Jesus is to know something or someone to be true, to trust that something and someone, and to 'act' on that knowledge and trust. It is the Gospel of John that emphasizes the term 'faith' or its verbal form 'to believe' the most, and there the same ideas are present. To 'believe' in Jesus is to know about him, to trust in him, to abide in him, to ingest his body and blood, and to act upon it all. At the time of Jesus, to 'believe' in Jesus was to 'associate oneself with him'. For many, of course, this would be a 'kiss of death' or at least a 'kiss goodbye' and perhaps a 'bop on the kisser'. Because Jesus was a magnet of opposition, association with Jesus meant social tension and sometimes ostracism or martyrdom. This is why Jesus finds it necessary to bless 'those who are persecuted in the cause of right' (p. 93) and why he also calls his followers that

'Anyone who wishes to be a follower of mine must renounce self; he must take up his cross and follow me' (p. 117).

Repentance as 'returning home to the father' and faith as 'association with Jesus' brings to the fore the fundamental 'personal' nature of the kingdom for Jesus. Humans are persons who are made of heart, soul, mind and body, and not just minds. To 'repent' or to 'believe' is a deeply personal act by one person toward another. Tenets of faith play a central role in any religion, but tenets can be overrated. In the hands of the wrong persons, they become not windows onto the deeper realities but instruments of power and boundary-making. As the essayist William Hazlitt has said, tenets are more of a 'map' than a 'picture' of the world we live in.[7] Jesus gave to his followers a 'kingdom' map and then filled it with parabolic pictures, and the primary picture he painted was about love of God and others.

Love

It is because his 'kingdom' vision is a deeply personal relationship both with God and others that Jesus can let *everything he believes about discipleship and ethics* settle down into 'love'. To understand the context of the so-called Great Commandment, which is really (as *The Story of the Christ* properly has it) 'the two great commandments', we need to recall that every day the pious Jew both begins and ends the day, among other times – like leaving the house or entering the house – by reciting the sacred *Shema*. And, there were at the time of Jesus discussions and debates about the most important commandment of all, and it was a process of deciding which of the 613 commandments or prohibitions was the most central. So, it is not surprising that Jesus is asked that very question (p. 155):

> Then one of the scribes, who had been listening to these discussions and had observed how well Jesus answered, came forward and asked him, 'Which is the first of all the commandments?'

Jesus responds with both a critique and an answer. There is not 'just one' he seems to be saying. 'But, since you ask that sort of question,' he is stating, 'you know the answer and I'll just give it a little twist to amend it.'

> The first is, 'Hear, Israel: the Lord is our God, the Lord our one God, and you must love the Lord your God with all your heart and with all your soul and with all your mind [*this is not in Deuteronomy 6*], and with all your strength.' The second [*and this is from Leviticus 19:18*] is this: 'You must love your neighbour as yourself.' No other commandment is greater than these.

In another of my books this 'amended creed' I call the 'Jesus creed'. When asked what is the greatest of all the commandments, Jesus creates a twofold challenge for all those who would follow him: it is about loving God *and* loving others. The obvious feature of this statement of Jesus is that he has 'amended' the *Shema* by adding 'love others' to 'love God'. The text chosen by Jesus is from Leviticus 19:18. It should be noted that this 'new creed' of Jesus, called a 'new commandment' in John 13:34–35, is both very Jewish and still 'new' because, as most of us know from experience, 'sacred creeds' are amended only after debates and arguments. It took some *chutzpah* on Jesus' part to 'amend' the sacred creed of Judaism. Why?

Some in Jesus' world, as in ours, found it easier to love God than to love others. We can return to a parable we used earlier to illustrate Jesus' harsh words for the priestly establishment. In the parable of the good Samaritan, Jesus 'tells on' the priest and Levite (a temple assistant). When these two are descending on the road from Jerusalem to Jericho they happen upon a body on the road, and they think (as anyone would have) that the body is that of a dead man. Because they are priests, they know that they are not to 'defile' themselves by touching dead bodies. This commandment is found in the *Torah*, at Numbers 19:11–22. And so, in faithfulness to the *Torah*, they pass by the man. But, a

Samaritan (who is a stereotyped symbol for a religious hybrid) sees the same body, reads the same *Torah*, and stops, cares for him, lugs him down to an inn, and takes care of all his expenses. For Jesus, the behaviour of the priest and Levite, however much directed by *Torah*, is unacceptable. Why? Because 'love for God' is not at the expense of 'love for others'. For Jesus, one loves God *by* loving others, even if loving others is not a substitute for loving God. His followers are to be noted by observing both.

As Jews recited the *Shema* throughout the day as a daily reminder of their sacred obligation before God, so it appears Jesus expected his followers to do the same with this 'Jesus creed'. Evidence that early Christians recited the 'Jesus creed' can be found in Galatians 5 and 1 Corinthians 13, where Leviticus 19:18 – Jesus' specific addition to the *Shema* – shows up as central to Christian living. What Jesus gives in the 'Jesus creed' is a handle on the *Torah* or its commandments: all commandments, Jesus teaches, are either 'love God' commandments or 'love others' commandments. Once one adopts this way of reading the *Torah* it all falls into place.

The implications of shaping life by the Jesus creed, the daily recital of the vocation to love God and to love others, are enormous, as are other themes in Jesus' teaching.

Justice

Justice is a good example, not only because it was important to Jesus but also because it is the foundation of many modern societies. A comparison of our world's perception of justice with Jesus' perception becomes a testing ground for understanding what Jesus was all about.

Justice, especially in the Western world, has often been reduced to the following factors: justice is a condition or a set of laws that focus on individual happiness, freedoms and rights. Such a sense of justice comes to us at the formative hands of philosophers like Jean-Jacques Rousseau and Immanuel Kant and John Stuart Mill, even if it has been seriously challenged by social theorists like Peter

Berger or John Rawls and theologians like Reinhold Niebuhr, John Howard Yoder, Stanley Hauerwas or Miroslav Volf. And, whether designed or not, most, especially in the West, think of freedom as the capacity to do whatever one likes as long as it does not hurt another person. In other words, humans are entitled to 'happiness', and to find that happiness they are constitutionally promised freedom and rights. Which leads to an emphasis on individual diversity, and, most of us would say, an overabundance of individualism and the need to hear a little more about 'community' and the 'common good' or the 'commonweal'.

So often today the concept of 'community' is challenged, sometimes with the best of intentions, by the language of 'individual freedoms' and 'personal rights'. Justice's concerns, as articulated in the West, are with tearing down the walls of traditions that restrict personal freedoms and creating conditions that provide for those individual freedoms and rights so persons can find 'happiness'. Consequently, the pursuit of 'justice' is either concerned with punishing those who have abused freedoms or the freedoms of others ('retributive' justice) or redressing the imbalances created by the systemic abuse of freedoms ('reparative' justice). Both pursuits of justice idealize their task as one of 'restorative' justice. The immediate question that comes to mind is whether or not 'happiness' is a sufficient 'end' for humans. But there is more than this to challenge the current perception of justice.

The modernist or postmodernist is entitled to ask two questions: first, what is the specific 'condition' to which we are aspiring in our pursuits of justice? Is that condition 'happiness' or 'freedom' or 'entitlements'? And, second, 'who' is the one who gets to define 'justice'? For, as many have been quick to point out, the person or system defining justice will fashion the sense of justice into a particular shape. Studies of justice show that there is no such thing as 'neutral justice', for each definition is constrained by its governing power. The reader of *The Story of the Christ* can ask, what is the meaning of 'justice' if Jesus does the defining?

The answer is close at hand: if humans are created by God to be *Eikons* by reflecting God's glory by loving God and loving others, then the only sense of justice Jesus knows flows from his 'creed'. Justice for Jesus is a set of conditions in which humans both love God and love others. The only true justice for Jesus is not shaped by 'individual' freedoms or 'personal' rights because humans are only 'free' when they surrender their rights (the 'self') to be what God made them to be: his glory-reflecting *Eikons*. For Jesus, one suspects that 'happiness' is being an *Eikon* of God in the kingdom of God. The 'kingdom' Jesus imagines for his followers is a kingdom that has this sense of justice, and humans will need to turn from their current ways to bring in that kingdom. It follows that for Jesus 'justice' is not primarily shaped by 'economic conditions' (as both Marx and capitalists think) but by interpersonal relations to God and to others. Jesus would ask his followers to live out his sense of 'kingdom justice' and to live it out in the face of opposition and other alternatives.

Forgiveness
Because the 'ethic' of Jesus is shaped by 'kingdom', 'repentance and faith', and by the 'Jesus creed' of loving God and others, and because all of this reveals the profound 'personal' dimension of spirituality for Jesus, it is not surprising that Jesus sees 'forgiveness' as another central virtue.

In the most sacred of all Christian prayers, the 'Our Father', Jesus teaches his followers to pray daily the following (p. 97):

'Forgive us the wrong we have done,
as we have forgiven those who have wronged us.'

Peter, once baffled by Jesus' attention to forgiveness, asked if he was to forgive someone as many as 'seven times' (p. 120). To which Jesus responds with an amazing parable (pp. 120–1). A king wanted to settle accounts and there was one man who owed him 'ten thousand talents' (a ridiculous amount exaggerated for effect), and the king forgave him his debt. But that man's fellow servant owed him a small amount and the forgiven man hauled his fellow servant off to jail. One hopes such things wouldn't occur in reality, but the possibility awakens in Jesus' hearers an opportunity to hear his teaching: God has forgiven humans their enormous load of sins, so they are to forgive their fellow humans their relatively light load of sins against one another. And here is where Jesus' focus on personal relations comes to the fore – Jesus teaches that if his followers don't forgive others, they won't be forgiven by God! Again, the point is this: loving God and loving others cannot be divorced from one another.

Forgiveness is a sign of love, and to love our neighbours means we are to forgive them even when it is the hardest thing a victim can possibly do. The 'upside' of forgiveness is the sort of 'kingdom' society it can create because forgiveness, at some level, is an assault on a sense of retributive and even reparative justice. Forgiveness of past wrongs is an attempt to end a cycle of violence, what the French scholar René Girard calls 'mimetic rivalry', and to replace in its stead an alternative loving society.[8]

The poor

Love of others is visibly demonstrated in concern for the marginalized and the poor. A 'kingdom' society shaped by the 'Jesus creed' is a society in which love shapes all relations, and abject poverty or marginalization drives voices from the table and out of the room, creating injustice. The 'poor' are for Jesus then not just the 'objects' of mercy and benevolence, but the visible indicator of how much *shalom* or 'justice' is inherent to a given society. But, because Jesus knows that the new 'kingdom society' must not only be talked about but also 'embodied', he invites the 'poor' to his table and centres them as agents of power in the kingdom.

Readers of *The Story of the Christ* may be shocked at the frequency with which Jesus brings up concern for the outcasts of his society, but it all begins with his mother, Mary, a woman adored by Roman Catholics and Eastern Orthodox but virtually ignored by most Protestants. One wonders if one of the lines from Mary's famous song, sung at Christmas with the name of the *Magnificat* (pp. 67–8), should be translated 'From this day forward all generations [except Protestants] will count me blessed'!

Mary, as has been observed by scholars, belonged to a class of Jews called the *Anawim* ('the pious poor').[9] The *Anawim* are noted by three features: they are socially destitute and suffer on account of their poverty; they gather frequently round the Temple to express both frustration and hope; and they yearn for justice and the coming of the Messiah to establish that justice. Simeon and Anna (pp. 71–2) are also examples of *Anawim*. Mary's *Magnificat* illustrates a 'theology of liberation' for the class of persons to which she belonged: she exults when she senses that God is about to deliver Israel, and she sees this act of God in sending the Messiah to be a climactic measure of God's faithfulness to his covenant with Israel – his act will strip the mighty of their power and the wealthy of their riches as it clothes the *Anawim* with justice and fills their bellies with nourishment. It is this 'hand that rocked Jesus' crib' – and it is from Mary that Jesus developed a vision of the kingdom that meant justice for the poor. *Shalom* cannot exist when persons are marginalized.

The list of the 'marginalized' includes not only the economically impoverished but also 'the poor [in spirit]' (p. 93) as well as those who are marginalized by leprosy, demon possession, sickness and disease; those who are marginalized because they are female; those who were driven to the edges of society because they were widows (probably like Jesus' own mother); those who are marginalized because they were (for whatever reasons) driven to prostitution; and those who are driven to the fringes of society either because they were Gentiles or because they co-operated with Rome through the fluctuating but often enough oppressive taxation system.

Prayer

If Jesus learns from his father and mother to begin his day with the *Shema* as he amends it into the 'Jesus creed', he also learns from them that prayer is a feature of Israelite faith. Prayer by definition is when humans communicate in utter truthfulness with God.

By the time of Jesus, the prayers of Israel had been set into the form we now find in the Psalms. This collection of prayers was to the Jews what the Book of Common Prayer is to the Anglican, what the Missal or Breviary is to the Roman Catholic, and what the Divine Liturgy book is to the Eastern Orthodox.

Alongside the *Shema*, the pious Jew prayed other prayers, including something not unlike what is now called the *Amidah* – also called the *Ha-Tephillah* or the *Shemoneh Esrei*.[10] This is a set of eighteen benedictions, and it is quite likely that Jews prayed something like this in the first century CE three times a day – along with the *Shema* in the morning and evening, and at 'midday prayers' around 3 p.m. Since we don't have the form of this prayer from the time of Jesus, we can only guess, but we can reasonably assume (if the later versions are any indicator) that it included such things as gratitude for God's election and his gift of the *Torah* and the knowledge it gives to Israel, requests for forgiveness, as well as urgent prayers for Israel's deliverance and the establishment of the kingdom.

Not all prayers are (or were) set for Jews or for Jesus. As one reads through the Gospels, one frequently enough finds Jesus seeking solitude for prayer, and he seems to be specially intentional about prayer before major events in his own life. He is praying at his baptism, at his Transfiguration, and before his death as he contemplates the unravelling of life on his knees in Gethsemane. Jesus calls his disciples to 'honest' prayer, and exhorts them to 'keep it plain and simple' (p. 96): 'In your prayers do not go babbling on like the heathen . . . Do not imitate them, for your Father knows what your needs are before you ask him.' In particular, he exhorts his followers in strong language not to 'make a show' of their public prayers. If they are tempted to do that, he exhorts them to stay at home and 'go into a room by yourself' and take care of it in private.

The 'Our Father' is a case in point. First, the prayer is built on what is today called the *Kaddish* ('sanctification'), a Jewish liturgical prayer now associated with funerals. That prayer (in at least one of its versions) goes like this:

> Magnified and sanctified be his great name in the world he created according to his will. May he establish his kingdom during your life and during your days, and during the life of all the house of Israel, speedily and in the near future. And say Amen.

Even if this was not the specific form of the prayer in Jesus' time, it seems as though it, or something very similar, was in his mind when he was asked by his disciples to give them a prayer to use (Luke 11:1). The 'Our Father' and the *Kaddish* are similar in length and topics – the name of God being hallowed/sanctified; the kingdom of God coming; and the will of God. They are too close in such matters to think that the two prayers are not somehow connected.

Jesus gives his followers a prayer that is much like the *Kaddish*, but, just like with the *Shema*, he puts his own stamp on it. To the *Kaddish*, he adds another set of prayers that are concerned with others:

> 'Give us today our daily bread.
> Forgive us the wrong we have done,
> as we have forgiven those who have wronged us.
> And do not put us to the test,
> but save us from the evil one.'

If the 'Jesus creed' is the centre of Jesus' vision of spirituality, then the 'Our Father' is what happens to 'loving God, loving others' when it morphs into prayer. That is, if one loves God, one prays for God's name, God's kingdom, and God's will; and if one loves others, one prays for physical sustenance, spiritual forgiveness and moral fidelity.

In the version of the 'Our Father' that many have learned to recite, the closing lines are: 'for thine is the kingdom, the power, and the glory for ever and ever'. But these lines are not in the earliest manuscripts of the Gospels, so many translations today either eliminate this closing off of the prayer or put it in a marginal note. (It does not appear in the version on p. 97.)

What also needs to be observed is that in Judaism the person who prayed did not finish her or his prayer off by saying 'Amen'. Instead, 'Amen', an Aramaic term meaning 'so be it', was repeated by all those who listened in on the prayer and who wanted to 'second' it by affirmation. It would strike first-century Jews as funny to hear modern pray-ers finish off their own prayer by announcing that they 'agree with what they have prayed'!

4 | WHAT WAS JESUS LIKE?

Having now considered the nature and reliability of our sources, having familiarized ourselves with what religion was like at the time of Jesus, and having explored the major themes of his teaching, we come at last to the question with which we began: What was Jesus like? What were his main characteristics? And what is it about him that explains why he made such a lasting impact?

One of the first characteristics an observer of Jesus encounters in the Gospels is his *confident freedom*. There is a measured 'wildness' about Jesus – to use C. S. Lewis' inimitable description of Aslan. G. K. Chesterton, when he chronicled his own conversion to faith in his book called *Orthodoxy*, once said this: 'And the more I considered Christianity, the more I found that while it had established a rule and order, the chief aim of that order was to give room for good things to run wild.'[11] This good sense of 'wildness', the freedom to do what he chooses and the confidence to carry it out, chases Jesus from one incident to another in the Gospels.

Which is not to say that Jesus was chaotic or crazy, but that he seemed to have a clear eye for what was going on around him and a resolute purpose to do just as that eye gave him sight to do. It was customary in Judaism to eat with your equals and to make sure your food was *kosher* – which means that it fell within the laws given in the book of Leviticus. It was also customary to make sure that the unobservant, those who didn't follow the food laws in Leviticus, didn't share meals with those who were keeping *kosher* and who were thus eating according to a social vision shaped by obedience to the constantly refreshed laws of ancient Israel. Jesus' opponents thought that by eating with the unobservant he was disregarding their traditions. So they pinned an age-old category on him: 'a friend of tax-collectors and sinners'. In fact, that same saying about Jesus (found in Matthew 11:19, p. 105) says they also labelled him a 'glutton and a drinker' (p. 105). G. K. Chesterton, who once said 'I wish there were more time to play' (and he was old and very fat at the time), also said of himself: 'I have never been anything so refined as a gourmet; so I am happy to say that I am still quite capable of being a glutton.'[12] That Chesterton was. But, because it was apparently untrue and potentially libellous to accuse Jesus of such things, this label must be understood in context: the words 'a glutton and a drinker' are a legal accusation derived from ancient Jewish legislation, now found in Deuteronomy 21:20. In that text a son is charged as 'a wastrel and a drunkard' which is a label for a specific kind of son: a *rebellious* son. In other words, 'a wastrel and a drunkard' are less a description of the specific things Jesus was accused of doing and more a legal accusation designed to get a legal judgement – stoning!

This label of being a 'rebellious son' stuck to Jesus because there was, in his opponents' view, something to it. Jesus, it may be said as an aspect of his 'wildness', had what the quintessentially American Benjamin Franklin once called an 'aversion to arbitrary power'.[13] Once when Jesus was speaking to his friends about demons and other such dark moving objects, his mother and brothers knocked on the door to fetch him home for dinner. To which he replied: 'Here [sitting here with me] are my mother and my brothers' (Mark 3:34). He once told one of his would-be followers that, if he was serious about being a disciple, there wasn't even time to bid *Adieu* to his family before they took off for ministry (Luke 9:57–62).

Freedom sometimes runs into the shoals of *hubris* with Jesus – at least as an outsider might see him. This characteristic of Jesus, which we can call hubris or confidence or self-consciousness or even *chutzpah*, leaps from nearly every page of the Gospels and is there for all to see. Thus, in the same conversation with the fellow who didn't have time to say *Auf wiedersehen* to his parents, Jesus was approached by a man who told him that he'd love to follow along with Jesus but that his father had died (or was about to die) and that he wanted to return home and take care of this most serious of Jewish religious obligations: burying one's father. Now it ought to be said here that burying one's father exempted Jews from normal religious obligations, like reciting two standard Jewish daily prayers, the *Shema* and the *Ha-Tephillah*. (This according to the *Mishnah*, tractate *Berakot* 3:1, a Jewish 'law-book' that codifies interpretations and practices in the fourth century CE.) What we read in the Gospels is that Jesus told the man who asked to go home to bury his father to let the 'dead bury their own dead'. No matter how you turn that one, something seemingly ugly becomes visible to the reader. Most biblical scholars see this response by Jesus to be the harshest thing he ever said; it might be. Even if not, it takes some real *chutzpah* to say things like this, and Jesus did say things like this. But what sort of person says things like this?

The same kind of *chutzpah* led Jesus to enter into the Temple and tip tables over topsy-turvy. Normal Jewish people didn't do things like this; or, at least, they only did it once. None of those who did things like this survived – and Jesus didn't. And that leads me to the third characteristic of Jesus: *he was a magnet for opposition*. Regardless of how much those who wrote the Gospels loved Jesus, worshipped Jesus, and called him 'Lord' (Luke does this especially), one can't help but notice how many people *didn't like him*. Take, for instance, the Pharisees. They thought Jesus was so untraditional that he was a danger and menace to *Torah* observance. When the prostitute anointed Jesus' feet with oil, a Pharisee thought Jesus, whose claim to be a prophet was evidently now only skin-deep, should have seen her for who she was and told her to knock it off (p. 105). Jesus responded by defending the woman's action and suggesting that her oil was being put to a new use and into a new sacred service. The Pharisee didn't know quite what to make of Jesus.

It was the Pharisees' concern with *kosher* food and with correct table fellowship that led them into conflict with Jesus and what they considered to be his rather loose table associations. (By the way, there is no evidence that Jesus was eating non-kosher food like pork or shrimp or catfish.) It is the Pharisees' grumbling that Jesus eats with 'sinners' that prompts Jesus to tell the story of the prodigal son (pp. 130–1). This story is about a younger son who demands his inheritance early, and who takes that inheritance off to the Diaspora only to waste it on whores and unholy living. When the son comes to his senses, an image for 'repentance', he returns home to find a waiting, welcoming and forgiving father. He also observes that his older brother is anything but welcoming. This is all stereotype that makes for a good story. It is likely that the Pharisees failed to see that it was they whom Jesus was typecasting as the 'elder son' who begrudged the father's forgiveness. In effect, the problem with Jesus was that he was telling a 'new story' about Judaism, and the story he was telling was not the same story that the Pharisees were telling. His story was that God was breaking into history with the final kingdom, and that he was the one appointed by God to lead Israel into that kingdom. That kingdom would be populated by both the observant and the non-observant, if only they repented and gathered themselves round Jesus. His claims led to heated debate.

But it wasn't just the Pharisees who opposed Jesus. The Sadduccees, who were the elite of Jerusalem, didn't like him either. After all, he wasn't cautious in his comments about their superiors, the Romans. Jesus once called Herod Antipas a 'fox' – and he wasn't speaking about his sleek appearance (p. 127). The Sadducees had known since they were children that priests were not to defile themselves by touching a dead body, so when they come upon what looks like a dead body on the path, they avoid it. Jesus found such a practice unacceptable because it meant neglecting people bruised and at the point of death. This practice, and the priestly pride that accompanied it, he memorializes in the parable of the good Samaritan (p. 123). It didn't help Jesus' relations with the Sadduccees that his cousin, John the Baptist, the son of a priest, was beheaded by a Roman authority or that this same John had a firm belief that purity was to be established through baptism and not through the Temple. Jesus, by all appearances, was one of John's followers, or at least associates, for some time.

Jesus' comments to those who opposed him – whether Pharisee or Sadducee – didn't engender friendly relations between them, but, to borrow words from James Thurber, 'there was a lot of jabber then' and it probably went back and forth often.[14] What this all means, for one thing, is that the image of a 'nice religious boy' from Galilee can't be used for Jesus. Even if some thought he was 'nice', there were plenty who thought he was more 'nuts' than 'nice'. A stubborn fact of the Gospel records is that lots of people didn't like Jesus, and he was crucified in part because some of those people had the will and the power to silence him.

The next two characteristics of Jesus help to explain why it was that Jesus was a magnet of opposition: he was an *activist* and he was given to preaching. If we compare Jesus to Socrates, Plato, the Apostle Paul, the author of Hebrews, or to Augustine, we have one very notable feature: they were, each in their own way, intellectual types. Socrates and Augustine loved to chat about theory and about philosophical ideas, and each liked to work at long, at times somewhat cumbersome, argumentation. Not so for Jesus.

That is to say, as an *activist*, he gathered people round him, he organized, he orchestrated, and he had a plan to convert the nation to his vision of the kingdom of God. Here's how it worked. When Jesus went into a village, he evidently knew how to find people who would respond and who would support him while there. This is why he can instruct his disciples how to do this (p. 101). He would then address people, motivate them to consider the cost (p. 129), call them to follow him, and then he moved on to the next village (p. 101).

One of Jesus' main activities was preaching. When Matthew summarizes the ministry of Jesus decades later, he uses three terms: Jesus went around villages teaching, preaching and healing (Matthew 4:23–5; 9:35; 11:1). And, of all the things people remembered about Jesus, clearly it was his sermons and teachings that made the biggest impact. Those who heard Jesus would have connected Jesus to Israel's famous 'prophets', whose sermons were also remembered and collected into a set of books. Matthew recorded five of Jesus' sermons, though most today think Matthew has supplemented a sermon with other statements of Jesus about the same topics. These five 'sermons' are found in Matthew 5—7, 10, 13, 18, 23—25 – no fewer than nine chapters of little more than 'red letter' collections of sayings of Jesus. Those five sermons are called the Sermon on the Mount, the Mission Discourse, the Parable Discourse, the Church Discourse, and the Sermon on Mount Olivet. They are some of the most memorable things Jesus ever said.

Jesus is at his best with people, in telling stories about people, and in speaking clearly and forcefully about real-life situations. For some present-day followers of Jesus, familiarity with the Gospels, and with Jesus and the Christian tradition, can blunt what is the most distinctive feature of his teachings: the parables. You can read Plato or, worse yet, you can read Aristotle – who had the writing style of a chemist at work in a mortuary – and you won't find stories, or at least not enough of them. Apart from Augustine's own *Confessions*, he didn't tell enough stories, and Paul's most influential writing, the letter to the Romans, is entirely theological and (if truth be told) complicated in argumentation. But the Gospels are laced together by stories. Jesus' style was active, rather than pensive, contemplative, deliberative, argumentative and complicated. He didn't sit in rooms and read books and then pop open the door with a journal article for the intellectual elite. No, he read the book of nature and told stories about people. He could tell these stories because he had spent time with people – partly in Sepphoris, partly in Nazareth, partly in the surrounds of the Sea of Galilee, and partly in Jerusalem. He had seen, and he had observed. And the stories he told at times stung his audiences. There is an ongoing, however silent, discussion in the pages of *The Story of the Christ* – it is the discussion of 'who's on the right side with respect to Jesus' and Jesus tells his stories to flesh out that discussion. And sometimes they are subtle.

Jesus is on a mission to restore Israel, and he is being opposed. His weapon is to preach about it and he tells stories to make it clear to others what is really going on. When he senses the wind of opposition, instead of opening his sails to fly away, he lowers his nose and heads right into it. For Jesus, there is no looking back. He sets his sight on Jerusalem, enters the sacred Temple, tips over tables, and then when asked about his behaviour, he gives his audience a memorable, breathtaking story (pp. 152):

> There was a landowner who planted a vineyard [Israel?]: he put a wall around it [Temple?] . . . then he let it out to vine-growers [opponents!] . . . When the harvest season approached, he sent his servants to the tenants to collect the produce . . . But they seized his servants, thrashed one, killed another, and stoned a third . . . . Finally he sent his son . . . So they seized him, flung him out of the vineyard, and killed him.

So far, a good story. But Jesus forces his hearers to run the gauntlet – whose side are they on? Are they with the 'son' or are they with the vine-growers? Of course, they think, they are with the 'son' who was obviously treated unjustly. But, no, Jesus points out that he is the 'son' and that the vine-growers are the leaders of Jerusalem – chief priests and Pharisees. Those who took the time to listen to him recognized in Jesus' story not some moral tale but a devastating critique of their attitude toward his mission to bring the kingdom of God. Unlike the Zealots, the 'sword' of Jesus was the revealing word, usually told in story form.

What this should also make us realize is that Jesus' active life of preaching was not a life of *writing*. We don't have a single word that he wrote. No one even knows what Jesus wrote in the sand when some opponents thought they had him cornered after speaking to a woman who had been caught *en flagrant* (John 7:53–8:11)! That is, what we see in Jesus is a person who was 'out and about' speaking, talking, watching, listening and making shrewd comments and offering extended clarifications. Even though Jesus wasn't a writer, he showed all the signs of good writing: he had clear thoughts, he gathered them all together, put them in single file, and directed their march before his audience's eyes.

One inescapable feature of Jesus' preaching stands out and deserves to be seen as a characteristic of Jesus: *he hated hypocrisy*. Michel de Montaigne, that most eloquent and self-contained of French writers, opens up for us something Jesus was himself doing: 'In truth it is right to make a great distinction between the faults that come from our weakness and those that come from our malice.'[15] Some of our greatest writers, like H. L. Mencken, have focused too narrowly on the limits of humans, on their weaknesses, and make mush of human nature. But what Jesus exposed in his diatribes against hypocrisy was not weakness but malice, and he found it lurking far too often among the leaders who were responsible for the condition of those dependent upon them. We should remember that what Jesus is against is not 'Judaism' *per se* but a Judaism abused by some leaders.

We can begin with the observation that Jesus despised the ostentatious practice of religious acts, and he regularly let its practitioners know it. When Lord Middleton invited two young women, cousins at that, home without informing his dear wife, Jane Austen (in *Sense and Sensibility*) informs us of the following:[16]

As it was impossible, however, now to prevent their coming, Lady Middleton resigned herself to the idea of it with all the philosophy of a well-bred woman, contenting herself with merely giving her husband a gentle reprimand on the subject five or six times every day.

It might be observed that Jesus had the same apparent approach to 'helping' hypocrites to see their failings. One reads his power-ful critiques in the Sermon on the Mount, in Mark 7 (pp. 114–15) when Jesus points out that the fastidiousness with respect to washed hands needs to be met with an even more intense desire to be pure in heart, and in Jesus' last week he remonstrates at length with the Pharisees and scribes over their hypocrisies. What Jesus observed in certain leaders of his day can also be seen in our own times, including among leaders in the Church. Even if we are to make sure the same is not true of us, that does not mean that we don't at times think that Jesus 'got 'em good'. And we smile with approval, because the words he used carried their own punch. It would not be far from the mark to suggest that Flannery O'Connor's brilliant exposés of religious pretence, dressed up as they are in the grotesque images she chooses to employ, owe their origins to the ancient prophets of Israel, like Micah or Isaiah, and to Jesus' own excoriations in Matthew 23 (p. 125). Perhaps her own words best comment on Jesus': 'I doubtless hate', she wrote to Maryat Lee in June of 1957, 'pious language worse than you because I believe the realities it hides.'[17] The realities O'Connor believed in were those created by Jesus.

Wits, among whom I count Jesus, have a fairly good reputation in our society; and I am not talking about the zaniness that we find in David Letterman or Jonathan Ross or any other talk-show hosts. Such people are humourists or outright comedians. We are speaking here of the ability to say it all in memorable 'one-liners' that both strike home and make us wince or that make us smile (but not necessarily laugh).

As a wit, Jesus handed out his share of insults, one-line barbs that poke into the hearts of all of us, and he did so with a zest and jab that led to smiles and embarrassment all at once. So, when Jesus once healed on the Sabbath, and butted heads with those who thought he might be breaking the Sabbath commandments, he ended it all with a flourishing comment that put it all in perspec-tive: 'So, the Son of man is lord even of the Sabbath' (p. 85). When he did a little too much for the homefolk to stomach, Jesus said, 'A prophet never lacks honour except in his home town . . .' (Mark 6:4). And what was more potent and piercing than his comment to those who queried him about his disciples' cavalier disregard for hand-washing when he stated, ever so simply, '. . . by your tradition . . . you make God's word null and void' (Mark 7:13). While some of these one-liners are humorous, their intention was not to entertain but to reveal the human heart. What C. S. Lewis once said of Samuel Johnson can be said of Jesus: 'I don't know anyone who can settle a thing so well in half a dozen words.'[18] It is Jesus' sense of proportion that creates a space for his revelatory word to strike home.

It is not hard to see how Jesus' hatred of hypocrisy led to his becoming a 'magnet of opposition'. At the same time, of course, there were many, mostly among the humbler classes, for whom Jesus was a 'magnet of attraction'. In other words, he was *charismatic*. When reading *The Story of the Christ* it quickly becomes apparent that wherever Jesus is, a crowd gathers. We can see this when Jesus has to escape from the crowds in a boat because he is in such high demand (Mark 3) and when we are told that about 5,000 people gathered to hear Jesus teach (John 6). This is the definition of a charismatic person: someone who attracts others. People wanted to know what Jesus had to say on a variety of topics – hence the rather common practice in the Gospels of beginning a passage with something like 'and one time someone asked him . . .' or 'on another occasion, his disciples asked . . .'

In addition to being a magnet of attraction, Jesus' charisma extends to his being profoundly *spiritual*. Jesus was so known for his prayer that his disciples wanted in on the secret and asked him to teach them to pray. The most decisive indicator of a person's charismatic spirituality is the number of followers who both gather round that person and who follow his or her practices. Charismatic people draw people into themselves and into their practices of experiencing the divine. Jesus was no different; in particular, his prayer life and his healing ministry drew people to him.

There are many instances of Jesus praying in the Gospels. We have the 'Our Father' because, in part, the disciples of Jesus had seen Jesus pray and wanted to learn how to pray in the same manner (Luke 11:1–4). Jesus himself had several experiences that could be described as 'mystical' or 'visionary'. At his baptism he sees the Spirit descend as a dove (p. 75); he tells his disciples, 'I saw Satan fall, like lightning, from heaven' (p. 123), and he was mystically transfigured, or metamorphosed, before a small number of his disciples in Matthew 17 (p. 118).

In addition to his personal practice of prayer, Jesus' faith was such that, through his *healings,* he could somehow unleash the power of God for the benefit of others. Far too many Christians, reared as they are on the doctrines of the Church as formulated in the classical creeds beginning in the fourth century at Nicea and accustomed to think that Jesus is 'God', think that when Jesus healed others he was simply employing his 'divine nature' for the good of others. Without disputing the Christology of the Church (and I am a creedal Christian), it still needs to be observed that Jesus healed not by virtue of his 'deity' but by trusting in God for the power to be unleashed. As a deeply spiritual person, Jesus was 'in tune' with the Spirit and was in constant communion with God – through prayer, through trust, and through asking God to work through him. At least that is the impression one gets from reading *The Story of the Christ*.

One or two examples show that Jesus' own healing is a dimension, not of his 'nature' but of his spirituality. Jesus himself says 'But if it is by the Spirit of God that I drive out the devils . . .' (p. 106). In the Gospel of John, Jesus says that the Father loves the Son, and 'has given all things into his hand' (John 13:3) – which suggests that Jesus' power is the result of God's enablement.

Today, talk of 'miracles' raises concerns in many minds: are we to believe that Jesus *really* performed miracles? Since the days when empiricism made its way into the philosophical and religious world, influenced by such philosophers as Benedict de Spinoza, René Descartes and George Berkeley, many have defined a 'miracle' as an act of God that interrupts the laws of nature. However accurate that definition might be for some, the world of Jesus didn't see the miraculous as anything other than the 'way God did things'. The entire world and its operation were acts of a constantly acting God. And this God was both immanent and transcendent.

Having said this, it must be emphasized that 'miracle' is an interpretation of an otherwise inexplicable set of events. We use the term 'miracle' to explain a set of events, and we appeal to 'miracle' when we want to explain some set of events as the result of God's work. When John queries whether Jesus is who he says he is, Jesus appeals to what he has done – and these are miracles in any sense of the word (p. 104). And, it should be noted, Jesus sees these acts as demonstrations of the kingdom of God (p. 106) while John depicts them (in his interpretation) as 'signs' that point to God at work in Jesus and the new life he brings (pp. 77–8). 'Miracle' then is an explanation of a set of events, in the life of Jesus, that are best explained by appealing to God's powerful action. From the evidence, it is hard to deny that Jesus was one who healed, but that healing was a dimension of his spirituality.

Another characteristic of Jesus is that he was *zealous*. This actually provides the energizing force for his freedom, his hubris, his opposition, as well as for his activism and preachiness. What I mean here is that 'the man was on a mission'. Once the Pharisees thought they were doing a good turn for Jesus when they informed him that Herod Antipas was on to his case and would do to him what he had done to John the Baptist – and John had been summarily executed by decapitation. Jesus' response to the Pharisees reflects his steely determination, 'Go and tell that fox, "Listen: today and tomorrow I shall be driving out demons and working cures; on the third day I reach my goal." However, I must go on my way today and tomorrow and the next day, because it is unthinkable for a prophet to meet his death anywhere but in Jerusalem' (p. 127). Which being interpreted means this: 'Thanks Pharisees, but no thanks. Your words don't help me. My hands are in God's hands; Antipas can come after me but I am called by God and I will die with the other prophets in Jerusalem. And, by the way, he can look me up then and there because he will play a part in my death, but it won't be here in his territory.' So Jesus was, to use the language of Samuel Johnson, a person whose 'faculties are chained to a single object'.[19]

This focus of Jesus illustrates his zeal to do God's will. He could so many times have kicked back in Galilee, withdrawn to another sleepy village like Nazareth, and just bided his time until his opponents got over him. But he kept it up. When the opposition began, he simply threw fire on the gas by sending out the twelve to spread his good news about the kingdom (Mark 6:7–11) and then he tossed more gas on other fires by sending out the 72 (pp. 122–3). And when he knew the odds were stacked against him, he headed straight for Jerusalem and stuck his mouth in the head of the lion and challenged it to roar (p. 122). When he got there, he went to the heart of the city and took the heart out of the city: he staged a messianic entry (p. 151), tipped over tables, and got into verbal fisticuffs with one and all. He predicted the city's destruction and then sat down with his closest followers, established a meal of memory (p. 162–3), and set up an alternative means of access to God. (This is what is meant by 'taking the heart out of the city'.) His zeal here is indistinguishable from his freedom and *hubris*.

I ask forgiveness if the brush I have been using has tended so far to paint a picture of Jesus as a monochromatic zealous firebrand out to convert the world and to take on all challengers. I am persuaded that these are characteristics that stand out and would face any outsider who watched him from a distance. History, however, tells us a different, more nuanced story, and in part that story is different because it is told by insiders who knew the other side of Jesus: his heart, which was unusually big.

In all of these characteristics that we have so far examined we are missing a fundamental ingredient of Jesus' entire manner: his zeal was enveloped with *love* and *compassion*. He may have been zealous, and he may have been opposed, and he may have slammed the hammer down against hypocrisy, but you can't miss that this man was known for his loving acceptance of all sorts of people.

He was known for his table of fellowship. Every evening became a banquet, every night a symposium, every home a dining hall. And to the table came all sorts of marginalized folk: fishermen, Zealots, tax-collectors, prostitutes, lepers, demonized, and women aplenty. He did this because he believed God loved all people, and because he believed all humans – whether 'pure' or not, whether 'observant' or not, and whether morally sound or not – were made in God's image and, like Augustine after him, he knew that people weren't fully persons until they turned to God.

What, we can ask, do you think the Samaritan woman said about Jesus when she got home (pp. 79–80)? or the lepers who were healed when each of them got back home (p. 134)? or the poor man about whom Jesus told the story of Dives and Lazarus (p. 133)? or the woman caught in the act of whatever by whomever but who was suddenly freed for a new life (pp. 141–2)? The one line these people remember from Jesus were things like this: 'Be healed' or 'Be forgiven' or 'Be restored.' They remembered Jesus as someone who looked them in the eye, saw who and what they were, disregarded it because he knew who had made them, and invited them home. Jesus was for big tables in a big house, with places reserved for all sorts.

Jesus and the Judaism of his Day
Even when you have allowed for the Gospels having been written from a later, Christian perspective, it is difficult to escape the conclusion that Jesus was both *at home in Judaism* and at the same time *not completely comfortable with the Judaism of his day*.

Jesus was *at home in Judaism*; he spoke as if he thought like it, and he worshipped like it. His piety was Judaism's. He taught its themes, he told its stories, and he used its connections. With this consequence for all of us: until you and I understand

Judaism, we really can't get a good hold on Jesus. Until we understand '*Torah*' and 'purity' and 'Temple' and 'Land' and the like, we can't grasp what Jesus was saying and what he was doing. In other words, Jesus' mission was a 'Jewish' mission – a mission to Jews and for Jews and about Jews and in the terms of the Jews. His vision was rooted in Israel's scriptures, his God is the God of Israel's scriptures, his prophetic stance over against Israel is drawn from Israel's prophets, and his family – Joseph and Mary – and his extended family – John the Baptist, and his parents Zechariah and Elizabeth – are thoroughly Jewish and concerned with things Jewish. It is more than likely that Jesus worshipped at the Temple on High Holidays; he would have taken part in sacrificing lambs for Passover; he would have helped to build the 'tents' for *Sukkoth*; and he would have participated in synagogue services and the like in Nazareth. He was a Jew among Jews, and nothing he did or said (really ever) was anything but Jewish.

However, what he did and what he said created tensions – not because what he did or said was not Jewish but because it bucked the establishment and called for a new day.

In other words, Jesus was *not totally comfortable with the Judaism of his day*. He told this little parable, really little more than a wisdom riddle, and it went like this (with a little adjustment by me): 'No one but a dumb cluck puts new wine in an old wineskin' (p. 85). And that tells the whole story about Jesus: he came, not to break the *Torah* but to fulfil it, and he came not to tear apart the feasts of Israel but to set them on a new level – that is what the Lord's Supper is to *Pesach* – and he came not to abolish redemption but to restore it. So Jesus is himself the new wine in an old wineskin – he is (according to himself and to his followers) Jewish wine but cranked up so that the old wineskin of Judaism just can't contain his ferment. If you fill that wineskin with the juice that is Jesus, the skin will burst and the whole place will be a mess. And no one likes messes.

This not being comfortable with the Judaism of his day came to a head during the Feast of Unleavened Bread and Passover. Jesus entered the city of Jerusalem, went into the Temple courts, and started tipping over tables as an acted parable of what was about to happen to the Temple itself if the leaders refused to listen to him. By the end of the week he had been tried and summarily executed, on a cross, just outside the city. The Gospels tell us that Jesus not only predicted his death, but that his death would bring saving benefits to his followers. In one text, Jesus says that the 'Son of Man did not come to be served but to serve, and to give his life a ransom for many' (p. 137). And, along the same line of understanding, in the Last Supper, Jesus suddenly broke with the Passover custom and said, 'This is my body' and 'This is my blood, the blood of the covenant, shed for many for the forgiveness of sins' (p. 164). Jesus believed his death was beneficial; it was a death that absorbed violence, turned violence on its head, and brought kingdom redemption to his followers. From this point on, association with Jesus is association with the Crucified One and it furthermore means what Rowan Williams, the Archbishop of Canterbury, has so clearly said: 'God is known in and by the exercise of crucifying compassion; if we are like him in that, we know him.'[20]

Who then was Jesus?
It depends whom we ask. If we ask the opponents of Jesus, we would hear that Jesus is a *mamzer* (an illegitimate child; Mark 6:3; John 8:41) or a 'rebellious son' (p. 105) or a lawbreaker (p. 114) or a demonized person (p. 106) or a blasphemer (p. 84) or a false prophet and a deceiver (p. 105; p. 169), but they finally put him away with the charge that he claimed to be the 'King of the Jews' (p. 170). Should we ask them? Certainly.

What about the crowds? They evidently thought Jesus was a 'prophet'. Once they thought he was a great prophet (p. 88) and when he enters Jerusalem a similar idea crops up (p. 150). A Samaritan woman thought the same (p. 80) and so did a man whom Jesus had healed (pp. 144–5). The only reason Jesus can be charged with being a 'false prophet' is if someone else thought he was a true prophet (p. 169). But are they the ones to ask? Also, certainly. We'd want to know what everyone thought of Jesus.

How about if we ask Jesus what he called himself? It is surprising how infrequently readers pause to think this through. In the words of Henry David Thoreau, 'Public opinion is a weak tyrant compared with our own private opinion. What a man thinks of himself, that it is which determines, or rather indicates, his fate.'[21]

The most notable expression Jesus used to describe himself was 'the Son of Man'. For over a century scholars have disputed the precise meaning of 'Son of Man', and many have also argued that it is either entirely or partly a creation of the early Church – even though outside the Gospels the term almost never appears. This would create the unlikely scenario that the early Church created a term for Jesus that they chose (together) never to use except when they were writing Gospels!

No, the term comes right from the mouth of Jesus, but knowing this doesn't interpret it for us. The term 'Son of Man' is used in three senses in the Gospels. First, it is used in an 'earthly' sense. Here, the term is not unlike the way we use the term 'one' when we speak of ourselves as representative of others. Thus, in Mark 2:28 (p. 85) we read, 'so the Son of Man is lord even of the sabbath'. This most likely means 'those who follow Jesus are lord even of the sabbath' (or something like this).

A second sense is when 'Son of Man' is used for a figure who will suffer at the hands of others. In Mark 8:31 we read that, after Peter had declared Jesus to be Messiah, Jesus predicted his own death in these terms: 'Then he began to teach them that it was necessary for the Son of Man to suffer many things' (p. 117 has 'he').

A third and final sense is when 'Son of Man' refers to the symbolic figure first mentioned in the Old Testament book of Daniel (chapter 7), wherein there is a vision of one like a 'human being' (or 'son of man', as in most translations) who appears before the 'Ancient of Years' to be vindicated before all. Sometimes this is the sense of 'Son of Man' on the lips of Jesus. Thus: 'For the Son of Man is to come in the glory of his Father with his angels, and then he will give everyone his due reward' (p. 117).

Whatever one makes of the historical questions, in the Gospels Jesus constantly refers to himself through this rather ambiguous if also highly evocative expression of the 'Son of Man'. As one scholar has put it, the term functions as a 'job description' for Jesus' own mission as the true representative of the new Israel he is proclaiming in his kingdom message.[22]

Whatever one makes of the Gospels, the unavoidable questions always become, 'Who was Jesus?' and 'Why did Jesus meet the end he met?' And, right alongside those questions is this one: 'Why did the crucified Christ continue to exercise such influence – not only in the years immediately after his death but throughout the centuries, right down to our own day?'

*   *   *

We have now reached the end of our attempt to imagine Jesus as a first-century witness would have observed and reported him. The idea for approaching Jesus from the outside came from reading G. K. Chesterton's *The Everlasting Man*. In Part Two of this sometimes quite wonderful but always punchy book, he sought to describe Jesus from the point of view of an imaginary man from the moon who discovers the Gospels but had never heard of Jesus prior to reading them. Chesterton tells the truth about the Gospels with this: '. . . if we *could* read the Gospel reports as things as new as newspaper reports, they would puzzle us and perhaps terrify us much *more* than the same things as developed by historical Christianity . . . the moral is that the Christ of the Gospel might actually seem more strange and terrible than the Christ of the Church'.[23]

And so now I invite you to make up your own mind, as you turn the page and begin reading *The Story of the Christ*.

Part Two

THE STORY OF
THE CHRIST

PROLOGUE

In the beginning the Word already was.
The Word was in God's presence,
and what God was, the Word was.
He was with God at the beginning,
and through him all things came to be;
without him no created thing came into being.
In him was life,
and that life was the light of mankind.
The light shines in the darkness,
and the darkness has never mastered it.

The true light which gives light to everyone
was even then coming into the world.
He was in the world;
but the world, though it owed its being to him,
did not recognize him.
He came to his own,
and his own people would not accept him.
But to all who did accept him,
to those who put their trust in him,
he gave the right to become children of God,
born not of human stock,
by the physical desire of a human father,
but of God.

So the Word became flesh;
he made his home among us,
and we saw his glory,
such glory as befits the Father's only Son,
full of grace and truth.

1 | BIRTH AND EARLY YEARS

The Angel Gabriel Appears to Zechariah
In the reign of Herod king of Judaea there was a priest named
Zechariah, of the division of the priesthood called after Abijah. His
wife, whose name was Elizabeth, was also of priestly descent. Both
of them were upright and devout, blamelessly observing all the
commandments and ordinances of the Lord. But they had no children, for Elizabeth was barren, and both were well on in years.

Once, when it was the turn of his division and he was there to
take part in the temple service, he was chosen by lot, by priestly
custom, to enter the sanctuary of the Lord and offer the incense;
and at the hour of the offering the people were all assembled at
prayer outside. There appeared to him an angel of the Lord,
standing on the right of the altar of incense. At this sight,
Zechariah was startled and overcome by fear. But the angel said
to him, 'Do not be afraid, Zechariah; your prayer has been heard:
your wife Elizabeth will bear you a son, and you are to name him
John. His birth will fill you with joy and delight, and will bring
gladness to many; for he will be great in the eyes of the Lord. He
is never to touch wine or strong drink. From his very birth he will
be filled with the Holy Spirit; and he will bring back many
Israelites to the Lord their God. He will go before him as forerunner, possessed by the spirit and power of Elijah, to reconcile
father and child, to convert the rebellious to the ways of the righteous, to prepare a people that shall be fit for the Lord.'

Zechariah said to the angel, 'How can I be sure of this? I am an
old man and my wife is well on in years.' The angel replied, 'I am
Gabriel; I stand in attendance on God, and I have been sent to

speak to you and bring you this good news. But now, because you have not believed me, you will lose all power of speech and remain silent until the day when these things take place; at their proper time my words will be proved true.'

Meanwhile the people were waiting for Zechariah, surprised that he was staying so long inside the sanctuary. When he did come out he could not speak to them, and they realized that he had had a vision. He stood there making signs to them, and remained dumb.

When his period of duty was completed Zechariah returned home. His wife Elizabeth conceived, and for five months she lived in seclusion, thinking, 'This is the Lord's doing; now at last he has shown me favour and taken away from me the disgrace of childlessness.'

The Annunciation of the Birth of Jesus

In the sixth month the angel Gabriel was sent by God to Nazareth, a town in Galilee, with a message for a girl betrothed to a man named Joseph, a descendant of David; the girl's name was Mary. The angel went in and said to her, 'Greetings, most favoured one! The Lord is with you.' But she was deeply troubled by what he said and wondered what this greeting could mean. Then the angel said to her, 'Do not be afraid, Mary, for God has been gracious to you; you will conceive and give birth to a son, and you are to give him the name Jesus. He will be great, and will be called Son of the Most High. The Lord God will give him the throne of his ancestor David, and he will be king over Israel for ever; his reign shall never end.' 'How can this be?' said Mary. 'I am still a virgin.' The angel answered, 'The Holy Spirit will come upon you, and the power of the Most High will overshadow you; for that reason the holy child to be born will be called Son of God. Moreover your kinswoman Elizabeth has herself conceived a son in her old age; and she who is reputed barren is now in her sixth month, for God's promises can never fail.' 'I am the Lord's servant,' said Mary; 'may it be as you have said.' Then the angel left her.

Joseph's Dream

This is how the birth of Jesus Christ came about. His mother Mary was betrothed to Joseph; before their marriage she found she was going to have a child through the Holy Spirit. Being a man of principle, and at the same time wanting to save her from exposure, Joseph made up his mind to have the marriage contract quietly set aside. He had resolved on this, when an angel of the Lord appeared to him in a dream and said, 'Joseph, son of David, do not be afraid to take Mary home with you to be your wife. It is through the Holy Spirit that she has conceived. She will bear a son; and you shall give him the name Jesus, for he will save his people from their sins.' All this happened in order to fulfil what the Lord declared through the prophet: 'A virgin will conceive and bear a son, and he shall be called Emmanuel,' a name which means 'God is with us'. When he woke, Joseph did as the angel of the Lord had directed him.

Mary Visits Elizabeth

Soon afterwards Mary set out and hurried away to a town in the uplands of Judah. She went into Zechariah's house and greeted Elizabeth. And when Elizabeth heard Mary's greeting, the baby stirred in her womb. Then Elizabeth was filled with the Holy Spirit and exclaimed in a loud voice, 'God's blessing is on you above all women, and his blessing is on the fruit of your womb. Who am I, that the mother of my Lord should visit me? I tell you, when your greeting sounded in my ears, the baby in my womb leapt for joy. Happy is she who has had faith that the Lord's promise to her would be fulfilled!'

The Magnificat

And Mary said:

> 'My soul tells out the greatness of the Lord,
> my spirit has rejoiced in God my Saviour;
> for he has looked with favour on his servant,

lowly as she is.
From this day forward
all generations will count me blessed,
for the Mighty God has done great things for me.
His name is holy,
his mercy sure from generation to generation
toward those who fear him.
He has shown the might of his arm,
he has routed the proud and all their schemes;
he has brought down monarchs from their thrones,
and raised on high the lowly.
He has filled the hungry with good things,
and sent the rich away empty.
He has come to the help of Israel his servant,
as he promised to our forefathers;
he has not forgotten to show mercy
to Abraham and his children's children for ever.'

Mary stayed with Elizabeth about three months and then
returned home.

The Birth of John the Baptist

When the time came for Elizabeth's child to be born, she gave
birth to a son. Her neighbours and relatives heard what great
kindness the Lord had shown her, and they shared her delight.
On the eighth day they came to circumcise the child; and they
were going to name him Zechariah after his father, but his mother
spoke up: 'No!' she said. 'He is to be called John.' 'But', they said,
'there is nobody in your family who has that name.' They
enquired of his father by signs what he would like him to be
called. He asked for a writing tablet and to everybody's astonishment wrote, 'His name is John.' Immediately his lips and tongue
were freed and he began to speak, praising God. All the neighbours were overcome with awe, and throughout the uplands of
Judaea the whole story became common talk. All who heard it

were deeply impressed and said, 'What will this child become?' For indeed the hand of the Lord was upon him.

And Zechariah his father was filled with the Holy Spirit and uttered this prophecy:

'Praise to the Lord, the God of Israel!
For he has turned to his people and set them free.
He has raised for us a strong deliverer
from the house of his servant David.

'And you, my child, will be called Prophet of the Most High,
for you will be the Lord's forerunner, to prepare his way
and lead his people to a knowledge of salvation
through the forgiveness of their sins:
for in the tender compassion of our God
the dawn from heaven will break upon us,
to shine on those who live in darkness, under the shadow of death,
and to guide our feet into the way of peace.'

As the child grew up he became strong in spirit; he lived out in the wilderness until the day when he appeared publicly before Israel.

The Birth of Jesus

In those days a decree was issued by the emperor Augustus for a census to be taken throughout the Roman world. This was the first registration of its kind; it took place when Quirinius was governor of Syria. Everyone made his way to his own town to be registered. Joseph went up to Judaea from the town of Nazareth in Galilee, to register in the city of David called Bethlehem, because he was of the house of David by descent; and with him went Mary, his betrothed, who was expecting her child. While they were there the time came for her to have her baby, and she gave birth to a son, her firstborn. She wrapped him in swaddling clothes, and laid him in a manger, because there was no room for them at the inn.

Now in this same district there were shepherds out in the fields, keeping watch through the night over their flock. Suddenly an angel of the Lord appeared to them, and the glory of the Lord shone round them. They were terrified, but the angel said, 'Do not be afraid; I bring you good news, news of great joy for the whole nation. Today there has been born to you in the city of David a deliverer – the Messiah, the Lord. This will be the sign for you: you will find a baby wrapped in swaddling clothes, and lying in a manger.' All at once there was with the angel a great company of the heavenly host, singing praise to God:

'Glory to God in highest heaven,
and on earth peace to all in whom he delights.'

After the angels had left them and returned to heaven the shepherds said to one another, 'Come, let us go straight to Bethlehem and see this thing that has happened, which the Lord has made known to us.' They hurried off and found Mary and Joseph, and the baby lying in the manger. When they saw the child, they related what they had been told about him; and all who heard were astonished at what the shepherds said. But Mary treasured up all these things and pondered over them. The shepherds returned glorifying and praising God for what they had heard and seen; it had all happened as they had been told.

After Jesus's birth astrologers from the east arrived in Jerusalem, asking, 'Where is the new-born king of the Jews? We observed the rising of his star, and we have come to pay him homage.' King Herod was greatly perturbed when he heard this, and so was the whole of Jerusalem. He called together the chief priests and scribes of the Jews, and asked them where the Messiah was to be born. 'At Bethlehem in Judaea,' they replied, 'for this is what the prophet wrote: "Bethlehem in the land of Judah, you are by no means least among the rulers of Judah; for out of you shall come a ruler to be the shepherd of my people Israel."'

Then Herod summoned the astrologers to meet him secretly, and ascertained from them the exact time when the star had appeared. He sent them to Bethlehem, and said, 'Go and make a careful search for the child, and when you have found him, bring me word, so that I may go myself and pay him homage.'

After hearing what the king had to say they set out; there before them was the star they had seen rising, and it went ahead of them until it stopped above the place where the child lay. They were overjoyed at the sight of it and, entering the house, they saw the child with Mary his mother and bowed low in homage to him; they opened their treasure chests and presented gifts to him: gold, frankincense, and myrrh. Then they returned to their own country by another route, for they had been warned in a dream not to go back to Herod.

Eight days later the time came to circumcise him, and he was given the name Jesus, the name given by the angel before he was conceived.

Then, after the purification had been completed in accordance with the law of Moses, they brought him up to Jerusalem to present him to the Lord. There was at that time in Jerusalem a man called Simeon. This man was upright and devout, one who watched and waited for the restoration of Israel, and the Holy Spirit was upon him. It had been revealed to him by the Holy Spirit that he would not see death until he had seen the Lord's Messiah. Guided by the Spirit he came into the temple; and when the parents brought in the child Jesus to do for him what the law required, he took him in his arms, praised God, and said:

'Now, Lord, you are releasing your servant in peace,
according to your promise.
For I have seen with my own eyes
the deliverance you have made ready in full view of all nations:
a light that will bring revelation to the Gentiles
and glory to your people Israel.'

The child's father and mother were full of wonder at what was being said about him. Simeon blessed them and said to Mary his mother, 'This child is destined to be a sign that will be rejected; and you too will be pierced to the heart. Many in Israel will stand or fall because of him; and so the secret thoughts of many will be laid bare.'

There was also a prophetess, Anna the daughter of Phanuel, of the tribe of Asher. She was a very old woman, who had lived seven years with her husband after she was first married, and then alone as a widow to the age of eighty-four. She never left the temple, but worshipped night and day with fasting and prayer. Coming up at that very moment, she gave thanks to God; and she talked about the child to all who were looking for the liberation of Jerusalem.

The Flight into Egypt

An angel of the Lord appeared to Joseph in a dream, and said, 'Get up, take the child and his mother and escape with them to Egypt, and stay there until I tell you; for Herod is going to search for the child to kill him.' So Joseph got up, took mother and child by night, and sought refuge with them in Egypt, where he stayed till Herod's death. This was to fulfil what the Lord had declared through the prophet: 'Out of Egypt I have called my son.'

When Herod realized that the astrologers had tricked him he flew into a rage, and gave orders for the massacre of all the boys aged two years or under, in Bethlehem and throughout the whole district, in accordance with the time he had ascertained from the astrologers. So the words spoken through Jeremiah the prophet were fulfilled: 'A voice was heard in Rama, sobbing in bitter grief; it was Rachel weeping for her children, and refusing to be comforted, because they were no more.'

After Herod's death an angel of the Lord appeared in a dream to Joseph in Egypt and said to him, 'Get up, take the child and his mother, and go to the land of Israel, for those who threatened the child's life are dead.' So he got up, took mother and child with him, and came to the land of Israel. But when he heard that Archelaus had succeeded his father Herod as king of Judaea, he was afraid to go there. Directed by a dream, he withdrew to the region of Galilee, where he settled in a town called Nazareth. This was to fulfil the words spoken through the prophets: 'He shall be called a Nazarene.'

The Boy Jesus in the Temple
Now it was the practice of his parents to go to Jerusalem every year for the Passover festival; and when he was twelve, they made the pilgrimage as usual. When the festive season was over and they set off for home, the boy Jesus stayed behind in Jerusalem. His parents did not know of this; but supposing that he was with the party they travelled for a whole day, and only then did they begin looking for him among their friends and relations. When they could not find him they returned to Jerusalem to look for him; and after three days they found him sitting in the temple surrounded by the teachers, listening to them and putting questions; and all who heard him were amazed at his intelligence and the answers he gave. His parents were astonished to see him there, and his mother said to him, 'My son, why have you treated us like this? Your father and I have been anxiously searching for you.' 'Why did you search for me?' he said. 'Did you not know that I was bound to be in my Father's house?' But they did not understand what he meant. Then he went back with them to Nazareth, and continued to be under their authority; his mother treasured up all these things in her heart. As Jesus grew he advanced in wisdom and in favour with God and men.

2 | BAPTISM AND EARLY MINISTRY

John the Baptist

In the fifteenth year of the emperor Tiberius, when Pontius Pilate was governor of Judaea, when Herod was tetrarch of Galilee, his brother Philip prince of Ituraea and Trachonitis, and Lysanias prince of Abilene, during the high-priesthood of Annas and Caiaphas, the word of God came to John son of Zechariah in the wilderness. And he went all over the Jordan valley proclaiming a baptism in token of repentance for the forgiveness of sins, as it is written in the book of the prophecies of Isaiah:

> A voice cries in the wilderness,
> 'Prepare the way for the Lord;
> clear a straight path for him.'

Crowds of people came out to be baptized by him, and he said to them: 'Vipers' brood! Who warned you to escape from the wrath that is to come? Prove your repentance by the fruit you bear; and do not begin saying to yourselves, "We have Abraham for our father." I tell you that God can make children for Abraham out of these stones. Already the axe is laid to the roots of the trees; and every tree that fails to produce good fruit is cut down and thrown on the fire.'

The people asked him, 'Then what are we to do?' He replied, 'Whoever has two shirts must share with him who has none, and whoever has food must do the same.' Among those who came to be baptized were tax-collectors, and they said to him, 'Teacher, what are we to do?' He told them, 'Exact no more than the assessment.' Some soldiers also asked him, 'And what of us?' To them he said, 'No bullying; no blackmail; make do with your pay!'

The people were all agog, wondering about John, whether perhaps he was the Messiah, but he spoke out and said to them all: 'I baptize you with water; but there is one coming who is mightier than I am. I am not worthy to unfasten the straps of his sandals. He will baptize you with the Holy Spirit and with fire. His winnowing-shovel is ready in his hand, to clear his threshing-floor and gather the wheat into his granary; but the chaff he will burn on a fire that can never be put out.'

In this and many other ways he made his appeal to the people and announced the good news.

The Baptism of Jesus
Then Jesus arrived at the Jordan from Galilee, and came to John to be baptized by him. John tried to dissuade him. 'Do you come to me?' he said. 'It is I who need to be baptized by you.' Jesus replied, 'Let it be so for the present; it is right for us to do all that God requires.' Then John allowed him to come. No sooner had Jesus been baptized and come up out of the water than the heavens were opened and he saw the Spirit of God descending like a dove to alight on him. And there came a voice from heaven saying, 'This is my beloved Son, in whom I take delight.'

The Temptations
Full of the Holy Spirit, Jesus returned from the Jordan, and for forty days he wandered in the wilderness, led by the Spirit and tempted by the devil. During that time he ate nothing, and at the end of it he was famished. The devil said to him, 'If you are the Son of God, tell this stone to become bread.' Jesus answered, 'Scripture says, "Man is not to live on bread alone."'

Next the devil led him to a height and showed him in a flash all the kingdoms of the world. 'All this dominion will I give to you,' he said, 'and the glory that goes with it; for it has been put in my hands and I can give it to anyone I choose. You have only to do homage to me and it will all be yours.' Jesus answered him, 'Scripture says, "You shall do homage to the Lord your God and worship him alone."'

The devil took him to Jerusalem and set him on the parapet of the temple. 'If you are the Son of God,' he said, 'throw yourself down from here; for scripture says, "He will put his angels in charge of you," and again, "They will support you in their arms for fear you should strike your foot against a stone."' Jesus answered him, 'It has been said, "You are not to put the Lord your God to the test."'

So, having come to the end of all these temptations, the devil departed, biding his time.

The First Disciples

The next day John saw Jesus coming towards him. 'There is the Lamb of God,' he said, 'who takes away the sin of the world. He it is of whom I said, "After me there comes a man who ranks ahead of me"; before I was born, he already was. I did not know who he was; but the reason why I came, baptizing in water, was that he might be revealed to Israel.'

John testified again: 'I saw the Spirit come down from heaven like a dove and come to rest on him. I did not know him; but he who sent me to baptize in water had told me, "The man on whom you see the Spirit come down and rest is the one who is to baptize in Holy Spirit." I have seen it and have borne witness: this is God's Chosen One.'

The next day again, John was standing with two of his disciples when Jesus passed by. John looked towards him and said, 'There is the Lamb of God!' When the two disciples heard what he said, they followed Jesus. He turned and saw them following; 'What are you looking for?' he asked. They said, 'Rabbi,' (which means 'Teacher') 'where are you staying?' 'Come and see,' he replied. So they went and saw where he was staying, and spent the rest of the day with him. It was about four in the afternoon.

One of the two who followed Jesus after hearing what John said was Andrew, Simon Peter's brother. The first thing he did was to find his brother Simon and say to him, 'We have found the Messiah' (which is the Hebrew for Christ). He brought Simon to Jesus, who looked at him and said, 'You are Simon son of John; you shall be called Cephas' (that is, Peter, 'the Rock').

The next day Jesus decided to leave for Galilee. He met Philip, who, like Andrew and Peter, came from Bethsaida, and said to him, 'Follow me.' Philip went to find Nathanael and told him, 'We have found the man of whom Moses wrote in the law, the man foretold by the prophets: it is Jesus son of Joseph, from Nazareth.' 'Nazareth!' Nathanael exclaimed. 'Can anything good come from Nazareth?' Philip said, 'Come and see.' When Jesus saw Nathanael coming towards him, he said, 'Here is an Israelite worthy of the name; there is nothing false in him.' Nathanael asked him, 'How is it you know me?' Jesus replied, 'I saw you under the fig tree before Philip spoke to you.' 'Rabbi,' said Nathanael, 'you are the Son of God; you are king of Israel.' Jesus answered, 'Do you believe this because I told you I saw you under the fig tree? You will see greater things than that.' Then he added, 'In very truth I tell you all: you will see heaven wide open and God's angels ascending and descending upon the Son of Man.'

The Marriage at Cana
Two days later there was a wedding at Cana-in-Galilee. The mother of Jesus was there, and Jesus and his disciples were also among the guests. The wine gave out, so Jesus's mother said to him, 'They have no wine left.' He answered, 'That is no concern of mine. My hour has not yet come.' His mother said to the servants, 'Do whatever he tells you.' There were six stone water-jars standing near, of the kind used for Jewish rites of purification; each held from twenty to thirty gallons. Jesus said to the servants, 'Fill the jars with water,' and they filled them to the brim. 'Now draw some off,' he ordered, 'and take it to the master of the feast'; and they did so. The master tasted the water now turned into

wine, not knowing its source, though the servants who had drawn the water knew. He hailed the bridegroom and said, 'Everyone else serves the best wine first, and the poorer only when the guests have drunk freely; but you have kept the best wine till now.'

So Jesus performed at Cana-in-Galilee the first of the signs which revealed his glory and led his disciples to believe in him.

The First Journey to Jerusalem

After this he went down to Capernaum with his mother, his brothers, and his disciples, and they stayed there a few days. As it was near the time of the Jewish Passover, Jesus went up to Jerusalem. In the temple precincts he found the dealers in cattle, sheep, and pigeons, and the money-changers seated at their tables. He made a whip of cords and drove them out of the temple, sheep, cattle, and all. He upset the tables of the money-changers, scattering their coins. Then he turned on the dealers in pigeons: 'Take them out of here,' he said; 'do not turn my Father's house into a market.' His disciples recalled the words of scripture: 'Zeal for your house will consume me.' The Jews challenged Jesus: 'What sign can you show to justify your action?' 'Destroy this temple,' Jesus replied, 'and in three days I will raise it up again.' The Jews said, 'It has taken forty-six years to build this temple. Are you going to raise it up again in three days?'

Jesus and Nicodemus

One of the Pharisees, called Nicodemus, a member of the Jewish Council, came to Jesus by night. 'Rabbi,' he said, 'we know that you are a teacher sent by God; no one could perform these signs of yours unless God were with him.' Jesus answered, 'In very truth I tell you, no one can see the kingdom of God unless he has been born again.' 'But how can someone be born when he is old?' asked Nicodemus. 'Can he enter his mother's womb a second time and be born?' Jesus answered, 'In very truth I tell you, no one can enter the kingdom of God without being born from water and spirit. Flesh can give birth only to flesh; it is spirit that gives birth to spirit. You ought not to be astonished when I say, "You must all be born again." The wind blows where it wills; you hear the sound of it, but you do not know where it comes from or where it is going. So it is with everyone who is born from the Spirit.'

'How is this possible?' asked Nicodemus. 'You a teacher of Israel and ignorant of such things!' said Jesus. 'In very truth I tell you, we speak of what we know, and testify to what we have seen, and yet you all reject our testimony. If you do not believe me when I talk to you about earthly things, how are you to believe if I should talk about the things of heaven?

'No one has gone up into heaven except the one who came down from heaven, the Son of Man who is in heaven. Just as Moses lifted up the serpent in the wilderness, so the Son of Man must be lifted up, in order that everyone who has faith may in him have eternal life.

'God so loved the world that he gave his only Son, that everyone who has faith in him may not perish but have eternal life. It was not to judge the world that God sent his Son into the world, but that through him the world might be saved.'

Jesus and the Samaritan Woman
News now reached the Pharisees that Jesus was winning and baptizing more disciples than John; although, in fact, it was his disciples who were baptizing, not Jesus himself. When Jesus heard this, he left Judaea and set out once more for Galilee. He had to pass through Samaria, and on his way came to a Samaritan town called Sychar, near the plot of ground which Jacob gave to his son Joseph; Jacob's well was there. It was about noon, and Jesus, tired after his journey, was sitting by the well.

His disciples had gone into the town to buy food. Meanwhile a Samaritan woman came to draw water, and Jesus said to her, 'Give me a drink.' The woman said, 'What! You, a Jew, ask for a drink from a Samaritan woman?' (Jews do not share drinking vessels with Samaritans.) Jesus replied, 'If only you knew what God gives, and who it is that is asking you for a drink, you would have asked him and he would have given you living water.' 'Sir,' the woman said, 'you have no bucket and the well is deep, so where can you get "living water"? Are you greater than Jacob our ancestor who gave us the well and drank from it himself, he and his sons and his cattle too?' Jesus answered, 'Everyone who drinks this water will be thirsty again; but whoever drinks the water I shall give will never again be thirsty. The water that I shall give will be a spring of water within him, welling up and bringing eternal life.' 'Sir,' said the woman, 'give me this water, and then I shall not be thirsty, nor have to come all this way to draw water.'

'Go and call your husband,' said Jesus, 'and come back here.' She answered, 'I have no husband.' Jesus said, 'You are right in saying that you have no husband, for though you have had five husbands, the man you are living with now is not your husband. You have spoken the truth!' 'Sir,' replied the woman, 'I can see you are a prophet. Our fathers worshipped on this mountain, but you Jews say that the place where God must be worshipped is in Jerusalem.' 'Believe me,' said Jesus, 'the time is coming when you will worship the Father neither on this mountain nor in Jerusalem. You Samaritans worship you know not what; we worship what we know. It is from the Jews that salvation comes. But the time is coming, indeed it is already here, when true worshippers will worship the Father in spirit and in truth. These are the worshippers the Father wants. God is spirit, and those who worship him must worship in spirit and in truth.' The woman answered, 'I know that Messiah' (that is, Christ) 'is coming. When he comes he will make everything clear to us.' Jesus said to her, 'I am he, I who am speaking to you.'

At that moment his disciples returned, and were astonished to find him talking with a woman; but none of them said, 'What do you want?' or, 'Why are you talking with her?' The woman left her water-jar and went off to the town, where she said to the people, 'Come and see a man who has told me everything I ever did. Could this be the Messiah?' They left the town and made their way towards him.

Many Samaritans of that town came to believe in him because of the woman's testimony: 'He told me everything I ever did.' So when these Samaritans came to him they pressed him to stay with them; and he stayed there two days. Many more became believers because of what they heard from his own lips. They told the woman, 'It is no longer because of what you said that we believe, for we have heard him ourselves; and we are convinced that he is the Saviour of the world.'

Jesus Teaches in the Synagogue at Nazareth

Then Jesus, armed with the power of the Spirit, returned to Galilee; and reports about him spread through the whole countryside. He taught in their synagogues and everyone sang his praises. He came to Nazareth, where he had been brought up, and went to the synagogue on the sabbath day as he regularly did. He stood up to read the lesson and was handed the scroll of the prophet Isaiah. He opened the scroll and found the passage which says,

> 'The spirit of the Lord is upon me
> because he has anointed me;
> he has sent me to announce good news to the poor,
> to proclaim release for prisoners
> and recovery of sight for the blind;
> to let the broken victims go free,
> to proclaim the year of the Lord's favour.'

He rolled up the scroll, gave it back to the attendant, and sat down; and all eyes in the synagogue were fixed on him.

He began to address them: 'Today', he said, 'in your hearing this text has come true.' There was general approval; they were astonished that words of such grace should fall from his lips. 'Is not this Joseph's son?' they asked. Then Jesus said, 'No doubt you will quote to me the proverb, "Physician, heal yourself!" and say, "We have heard of all your doings at Capernaum; do the same here in your own home town." Truly I tell you,' he went on: 'no prophet is recognized in his own country. There were indeed many widows in Israel in Elijah's time, when for three and a half years the skies never opened, and famine lay hard over the whole country; yet it was to none of these that Elijah was sent, but to a widow at Sarepta in the territory of Sidon. Again, in the time of the prophet Elisha there were many lepers in Israel, and not one of them was healed, but only Naaman, the Syrian.' These words roused the whole congregation to fury; they leapt up, drove him out of the town, and took him to the brow of the hill on which it was built, meaning to hurl him over the edge. But he walked straight through the whole crowd, and went away.

The First Healings
Coming down to Capernaum, a town in Galilee, he taught the people on the sabbath, and they were amazed at his teaching, for what he said had the note of authority. Now there was a man in the synagogue possessed by a demon, an unclean spirit. He shrieked at the top of his voice, 'What do you want with us, Jesus of Nazareth? Have you come to destroy us? I know who you are – the Holy One of God.' Jesus rebuked him: 'Be silent', he said, 'and come out of him.' Then the demon, after throwing the man down in front of the people, left him without doing him any injury. Amazement fell on them all and they said to one another: 'What is there in this man's words? He gives orders to the unclean spirits with authority and power, and they go.' So the news spread, and he was the talk of the whole district.

On leaving the synagogue he went to Simon's house. Simon's mother-in-law was in the grip of a high fever; and they asked him to help her. He stood over her and rebuked the fever. It left her, and she got up at once and attended to their needs.

At sunset all who had friends ill with diseases of one kind or another brought them to him; and he laid his hands on them one by one and healed them. Demons also came out of many of them, shouting, 'You are the Son of God.' But he rebuked them and forbade them to speak, because they knew he was the Messiah.

The Miraculous Catch of Fish
One day as he stood by the lake of Gennesaret, with people crowding in on him to listen to the word of God, he noticed two boats lying at the water's edge; the fishermen had come ashore and were washing their nets. He got into one of the boats, which belonged to Simon, and asked him to put out a little way from the shore; then he went on teaching the crowds as he sat in the boat. When he had finished speaking, he said to Simon, 'Put out into deep water and let down your nets for a catch.' Simon answered, 'Master, we were hard at work all night and caught nothing; but if you say so, I will let down the nets.' They did so and made such a huge catch of fish that their nets began to split. So they signalled to their partners in the other boat to come and help them. They came, and loaded both boats to the point of sinking. When Simon saw what had happened he fell at Jesus's knees and said, 'Go, Lord, leave me, sinner that I am!' For he and all his companions were amazed at the catch they had made; so too were his partners James and John, Zebedee's sons. 'Do not be afraid,' said Jesus to Simon; 'from now on you will be catching people.' As soon as they had brought the boats to land, they left everything and followed him.

The Cleansing of a Leper
On one occasion he was approached by a leper, who knelt before him and begged for help. 'If only you will,' said the man, 'you can make me clean.' Jesus was moved to anger; he stretched out his hand, touched him, and said, 'I will; be clean.' The leprosy left him immediately, and he was clean. Then he dismissed him with this stern warning: 'See that you tell nobody, but go and show yourself to the priest, and make the offering laid down by Moses for your cleansing; that will certify the cure.' But the man went

away and made the whole story public, spreading it far and wide, until Jesus could no longer show himself in any town. He stayed outside in remote places; yet people kept coming to him from all quarters.

The Healing of a Paralysed Man

After some days he returned to Capernaum, and news went round that he was at home; and such a crowd collected that there was no room for them even in the space outside the door. While he was proclaiming the message to them, a man was brought who was paralysed. Four men were carrying him, but because of the crowd they could not get him near. So they made an opening in the roof over the place where Jesus was, and when they had broken through they lowered the bed on which the paralysed man was lying. When he saw their faith, Jesus said to the man, 'My son, your sins are forgiven.'

Now there were some scribes sitting there, thinking to themselves, 'How can the fellow talk like that? It is blasphemy! Who but God can forgive sins?' Jesus knew at once what they were thinking, and said to them, 'Why do you harbour such thoughts? Is it easier to say to this paralysed man, "Your sins are forgiven," or to say, "Stand up, take your bed, and walk"? But to convince you that the Son of Man has authority on earth to forgive sins' – he turned to the paralysed man – 'I say to you, stand up, take your bed, and go home.' And he got up, and at once took his bed and went out in full view of them all, so that they were astounded and praised God. 'Never before', they said, 'have we seen anything like this.'

The Call of Levi

Once more he went out to the lakeside. All the crowd came to him there, and he taught them. As he went along, he saw Levi son of Alphaeus at his seat in the custom-house, and said to him, 'Follow me'; and he rose and followed him.

When Jesus was having a meal in his house, many tax-collectors and sinners were seated with him and his disciples, for there were many of them among his followers. Some scribes who were Pharisees, observing the company in which he was eating, said to his disciples, 'Why does he eat with tax-collectors and sinners?' Hearing this, Jesus said to them, 'It is not the healthy who need a doctor, but the sick; I did not come to call the virtuous, but sinners.'

New Wine in Old Wine Skins
Once, when John's disciples and the Pharisees were keeping a fast, some people came and asked him, 'Why is it that John's disciples and the disciples of the Pharisees are fasting, but yours are not?' Jesus replied, 'Can you expect the bridegroom's friends to fast while the bridegroom is with them? As long as he is with them, there can be no fasting. But the time will come when the bridegroom will be taken away from them; that will be the time for them to fast.

'No one sews a patch of unshrunk cloth on to an old garment; if he does, the patch tears away from it, the new from the old, and leaves a bigger hole. No one puts new wine into old wineskins; if he does, the wine will burst the skins, and then wine and skins are both lost. New wine goes into fresh skins.'

Lord of the Sabbath
One sabbath he was going through the cornfields; and as they went along his disciples began to pluck ears of corn. The Pharisees said to him, 'Why are they doing what is forbidden on the sabbath?' He answered, 'Have you never read what David did when he and his men were hungry and had nothing to eat? He went into the house of God, in the time of Abiathar the high priest, and ate the sacred bread, though no one but a priest is allowed to eat it, and even gave it to his men.'

He also said to them, 'The sabbath was made for man, not man for the sabbath: so the Son of Man is lord even of the sabbath.'

The Healing of a Man with the Withered Hand

On another sabbath he had gone to synagogue and was teaching. There was a man in the congregation whose right arm was withered; and the scribes and Pharisees were on the watch to see whether Jesus would heal him on the sabbath, so that they could find a charge to bring against him. But he knew what was in their minds and said to the man with the withered arm, 'Stand up and come out here.' So he stood up and came out. Then Jesus said to them, 'I put this question to you: is it permitted to do good or to do evil on the sabbath, to save life or to destroy it?' He looked round at them all, and then he said to the man, 'Stretch out your arm.' He did so, and his arm was restored. But they totally failed to understand, and began to discuss with one another what they could do to Jesus.

The Twelve Disciples

During this time he went out one day into the hill-country to pray, and spent the night in prayer to God. When day broke he called his disciples to him, and from among them he chose twelve and named them apostles: Simon, to whom he gave the name Peter, and Andrew his brother, James and John, Philip and Bartholomew, Matthew and Thomas, James son of Alphaeus, and Simon who was called the Zealot, Judas son of James, and Judas Iscariot who turned traitor.

Blessings and Warnings

He came down the hill with them and stopped on some level ground where a large crowd of his disciples had gathered. Turning to his disciples he began to speak:

'Blessed are you who are in need;
the kingdom of God is yours.
Blessed are you who now go hungry;
you will be satisfied.

Blessed are you who weep now;
you will laugh.

'But alas for you who are rich;
you have had your time of happiness.
Alas for you who are well fed now;
you will go hungry.
Alas for you who laugh now;
you will mourn and weep.
Alas for you when all speak well of you;
that is how their fathers treated the false prophets.

He also spoke to them in a parable: 'Can one blind man guide another? Will not both fall into the ditch? No pupil ranks above his teacher; fully trained he can but reach his teacher's level.'

The Healing of a Centurion's Servant
When he had finished addressing the people, he entered Capernaum. A centurion there had a servant whom he valued highly, but the servant was ill and near to death. Hearing about Jesus, he sent some Jewish elders to ask him to come and save his servant's life. They approached Jesus and made an urgent appeal to him: 'He deserves this favour from you,' they said, 'for he is a friend of our nation and it is he who built us our synagogue.' Jesus went with them; but when he was not far from the house, the centurion sent friends with this message: 'Do not trouble further, sir; I am not worthy to have you come under my roof, and that is why I did not presume to approach you in person. But say the word and my servant will be cured. I know, for I am myself under orders, with soldiers under me. I say to one, "Go," and he goes; to another, "Come here," and he comes; and to my servant, "Do this," and he does it.' When Jesus heard this, he was astonished, and, turning to the crowd that was following him, he said, 'I tell you, not even in Israel have I found such faith.' When the messengers returned to the house, they found the servant in good health.

The Raising of a Widow's Son
Afterwards Jesus went to a town called Nain, accompanied by his disciples and a large crowd. As he approached the gate of the town he met a funeral. The dead man was the only son of his widowed mother; and many of the townspeople were there with her. When the Lord saw her his heart went out to her, and he said, 'Do not weep.' He stepped forward and laid his hand on the bier; and the bearers halted. Then he spoke: 'Young man, I tell you to get up.' The dead man sat up and began to speak; and Jesus restored him to his mother. Everyone was filled with awe and praised God. 'A great prophet has arisen among us,' they said; 'God has shown his care for his people.' The story of what he had done spread through the whole of Judaea and all the region around.

The Parable of the Sower
On another occasion he began to teach by the lakeside. The crowd that gathered round him was so large that he had to get into a boat on the lake and sit there, with the whole crowd on the beach right down to the water's edge. And he taught them many things by parables.

As he taught he said: 'Listen! A sower went out to sow. And it happened that as he sowed, some of the seed fell along the footpath; and the birds came and ate it up. Some fell on rocky ground, where it had little soil, and it sprouted quickly because it had no depth of earth; but when the sun rose it was scorched, and as it had no root it withered away. Some fell among thistles; and the thistles grew up and choked the corn, and it produced no crop. And some of the seed fell into good soil, where it came up and grew, and produced a crop; and the yield was thirtyfold, sixtyfold, even a hundredfold.' He added, 'If you have ears to hear, then hear.'

When Jesus was alone with the Twelve and his other companions they questioned him about the parables. He answered, 'To you the secret of the kingdom of God has been given; but to those who are outside, everything comes by way of parables, so that (as scripture says) they may look and look, but see nothing; they may listen and listen, but understand nothing; otherwise they might turn to God and be forgiven.'

He went on: 'Do you not understand this parable? How then are you to understand any parable? The sower sows the word. With some the seed falls along the footpath; no sooner have they heard it than Satan comes and carries off the word which has been sown in them. With others the seed falls on rocky ground; as soon as they hear the word, they accept it with joy, but it strikes no root in them; they have no staying-power, and when there is trouble or persecution on account of the word, they quickly lose faith. With others again the seed falls among thistles; they hear the word, but worldly cares and the false glamour of wealth and evil desires of all kinds come in and choke the word, and it proves barren. But there are some with whom the seed is sown on good soil; they accept the word when they hear it, and they bear fruit thirtyfold, sixtyfold, or a hundredfold.'

Two Parables of the Kingdom
He said, 'The kingdom of God is like this. A man scatters seed on the ground; he goes to bed at night and gets up in the morning, and meanwhile the seed sprouts and grows – how, he does not know. The ground produces a crop by itself, first the blade, then the ear, then full grain in the ear; but as soon as the crop is ripe, he starts reaping, because harvest time has come.'

He said, 'How shall we picture the kingdom of God, or what parable shall we use to describe it? It is like a mustard seed; when sown in the ground it is smaller than any other seed, but once sown, it springs up and grows taller than any other plant, and forms branches so large that birds can roost in its shade.'

With many such parables he used to give them his message, so far as they were able to receive it. He never spoke to them except in parables; but privately to his disciples he explained everything.

The Calming of the Storm

That day, in the evening, he said to them, 'Let us cross over to the other side of the lake.' So they left the crowd and took him with them in the boat in which he had been sitting; and some other boats went with him. A fierce squall blew up and the waves broke over the boat until it was all but swamped. Now he was in the stern asleep on a cushion; they roused him and said, 'Teacher, we are sinking! Do you not care?' He awoke and rebuked the wind, and said to the sea, 'Silence! Be still!' The wind dropped and there was a dead calm. He said to them, 'Why are you such cowards? Have you no faith even now?' They were awestruck and said to one another, 'Who can this be? Even the wind and the sea obey him.'

The Healing of a Madman

So they came to the country of the Gerasenes on the other side of the lake. As Jesus stepped ashore, a man possessed by an unclean spirit came up to him from among the tombs where he had made his home. Nobody could control him any longer; even chains were useless, for he had often been fettered and chained up, but had snapped his chains and broken the fetters. No one was strong enough to master him. Unceasingly, night and day, he would cry aloud among the tombs and on the hillsides and gash himself with stones. When he saw Jesus in the distance, he ran up and flung himself down before him, shouting at the top of his voice, 'What do you want with me, Jesus, son of the Most High God? In God's name do not torment me.' For Jesus was already saying to him, 'Out, unclean spirit, come out of the man!' Jesus asked him, 'What is your name?' 'My name is Legion,' he said, 'there are so many of us.' And he implored Jesus not to send them out of the district. There was a large herd of pigs nearby, feeding on the hillside, and the spirits begged him, 'Send us among the pigs; let us go into them.' He gave them leave; and the unclean spirits came out and went into the pigs; and the herd, of about two thousand, rushed over the edge into the lake and were drowned.

The men in charge of them took to their heels and carried the news to the town and countryside; and the people came out to see what had happened. When they came to Jesus and saw the madman who had been possessed by the legion of demons, sitting there clothed and in his right mind, they were afraid. When eye-witnesses told them what had happened to the madman and what had become of the pigs, they begged Jesus to leave the district. As he was getting into the boat, the man who had been possessed begged to go with him. But Jesus would not let him. 'Go home to your own people,' he said, 'and tell them what the Lord in his mercy has done for you.' The man went off and made known throughout the Decapolis what Jesus had done for him; and everyone was amazed.

The Healing of Jairus's Daughter and of a Woman who Suffered from Haemorrhages

As soon as Jesus had returned by boat to the other shore, a large crowd gathered round him. While he was by the lakeside, there came a synagogue president named Jairus; and when he saw him, he threw himself down at his feet and pleaded with him. 'My little daughter is at death's door,' he said. 'I beg you to come and lay your hands on her so that her life may be saved.' So Jesus went with him, accompanied by a great crowd which pressed round him.

Among them was a woman who had suffered from haemor-rhages for twelve years; and in spite of long treatment by many doctors, on which she had spent all she had, she had become worse rather than better. She had heard about Jesus, and came up behind him in the crowd and touched his cloak; for she said, 'If I touch even his clothes, I shall be healed.' And there and then the flow of blood dried up and she knew in herself that she was cured of her affliction. Aware at once that power had gone out of him, Jesus turned round in the crowd and asked, 'Who touched my clothes?' His disciples said to him, 'You see the crowd pressing round you and yet you ask, "Who touched me?"' But he kept looking around to see who had done it. Then the woman, trembling with fear because she knew what had happened to her, came and fell at his feet and told him the whole truth. He said to her, 'Daughter, your faith has healed you. Go in peace, free from your affliction.'

While he was still speaking, a message came from the president's house, 'Your daughter has died; why trouble the teacher any more?' But Jesus, overhearing the message as it was delivered, said to the president of the synagogue, 'Do not be afraid; simply have faith.' Then he allowed no one to accompany him except Peter and James and James's brother John. They came to the president's house, where he found a great commotion, with loud crying and wailing. So he went in and said to them, 'Why this crying and commotion? The child is not dead: she is asleep'; and they laughed at him. After turning everyone out, he took the child's father and mother and his own companions into the room where the child was. Taking hold of her hand, he said to her, '*Talitha cum*,' which means, 'Get up, my child.' Immediately the girl got up and walked about – she was twelve years old. They were overcome with amazement; but he gave them strict instructions not to let anyone know about it, and told them to give her something to eat.

3 | THE SERMON ON THE MOUNT

When Jesus saw the crowds he went up a mountain. There he sat down, and when his disciples had gathered round him he began to address them. And this is the teaching he gave:

The Beatitudes

'Blessed are the poor in spirit;
the kingdom of Heaven is theirs.
Blessed are the sorrowful;
they shall find consolation.
Blessed are the gentle;
they shall have the earth for their possession.
Blessed are those who hunger and thirst to see right prevail;
they shall be satisfied.
Blessed are those who show mercy;
mercy shall be shown to them.
Blessed are those whose hearts are pure;
they shall see God.
Blessed are the peacemakers;
they shall be called God's children.
Blessed are those who are persecuted in the cause of right;
the kingdom of Heaven is theirs.

'Blessed are you, when you suffer insults and persecution and calumnies of every kind for my sake. Exult and be glad, for you have a rich reward in heaven; in the same way they persecuted the prophets before you.'

Salt and Light
'You are salt to the world. And if salt becomes tasteless, how is its saltness to be restored? It is good for nothing but to be thrown away and trodden underfoot.

'You are light for all the world. A town that stands on a hill cannot be hidden. When a lamp is lit, it is not put under the meal-tub, but on the lampstand, where it gives light to everyone in the house. Like the lamp, you must shed light among your fellows, so that, when they see the good you do, they may give praise to your Father in heaven.'

The Completion of the Law
'Do not suppose that I have come to abolish the law and the prophets; I did not come to abolish, but to complete. Truly I tell you: so long as heaven and earth endure, not a letter, not a dot, will disappear from the law until all that must happen has happened. Anyone therefore who sets aside even the least of the law's demands, and teaches others to do the same, will have the lowest place in the kingdom of Heaven, whereas anyone who keeps the law, and teaches others to do so, will rank high in the kingdom of Heaven. I tell you, unless you show yourselves far better than the scribes and Pharisees, you can never enter the kingdom of Heaven.'

The Spirit of the Law
'You have heard that our forefathers were told, "Do not commit murder; anyone who commits murder must be brought to justice." But what I tell you is this: Anyone who nurses anger against his brother must be brought to justice. Whoever calls his brother "good for nothing" deserves the sentence of the court; whoever calls him "fool" deserves hell-fire. So if you are presenting your gift at the altar and suddenly remember that your brother has a grievance against you, leave your gift where it is before the altar. First go and make your peace with your brother; then come back and offer your gift. If someone sues you, come to terms with him

promptly while you are both on your way to court; otherwise he may hand you over to the judge, and the judge to the officer, and you will be thrown into jail. Truly I tell you: once you are there you will not be let out until you have paid the last penny.

'You have heard that they were told, "Do not commit adultery." But what I tell you is this: If a man looks at a woman with a lustful eye, he has already committed adultery with her in his heart. If your right eye causes your downfall, tear it out and fling it away; it is better for you to lose one part of your body than for the whole of it to be thrown into hell. If your right hand causes your downfall, cut it off and fling it away; it is better for you to lose one part of your body than for the whole of it to go to hell.

'They were told, "A man who divorces his wife must give her a certificate of dismissal." But what I tell you is this: If a man divorces his wife for any cause other than unchastity he involves her in adultery; and whoever marries her commits adultery.

'Again, you have heard that our forefathers were told, "Do not break your oath," and "Oaths sworn to the Lord must be kept." But what I tell you is this: You are not to swear at all – not by heaven, for it is God's throne, nor by the earth, for it is his footstool, nor by Jerusalem, for it is the city of the great King, nor by your own head, because you cannot turn one hair of it white or black. Plain "Yes" or "No" is all you need to say; anything beyond that comes from the evil one.

'You have heard that they were told, "An eye for an eye, a tooth for a tooth." But what I tell you is this: Do not resist those who wrong you. If anyone slaps you on the right cheek, turn and offer him the other also. If anyone wants to sue you and takes your shirt, let him have your cloak as well. If someone in authority presses you into service for one mile, go with him two. Give to anyone who asks; and do not turn your back on anyone who wants to borrow.'

Love Without Limits

'You have heard that they were told, "Love your neighbour and hate your enemy." But what I tell you is this: Love your enemies and pray for your persecutors; only so can you be children of your heavenly Father, who causes the sun to rise on good and bad alike, and sends the rain on the innocent and the wicked. If you love only those who love you, what reward can you expect? Even the tax-collectors do as much as that. If you greet only your brothers, what is there extraordinary about that? Even the heathen do as much. There must be no limit to your goodness, as your heavenly Father's goodness knows no bounds.'

True Religion

'Be careful not to parade your religion before others; if you do, no reward awaits you with your Father in heaven.

'So, when you give alms, do not announce it with a flourish of trumpets, as the hypocrites do in synagogues and in the streets to win the praise of others. Truly I tell you: they have their reward already. But when you give alms, do not let your left hand know what your right is doing; your good deed must be secret, and your Father who sees what is done in secret will reward you.

'Again, when you pray, do not be like the hypocrites; they love to say their prayers standing up in synagogues and at street corners for everyone to see them. Truly I tell you: they have their reward already. But when you pray, go into a room by yourself, shut the door, and pray to your Father who is in secret; and your Father who sees what is done in secret will reward you.

'In your prayers do not go babbling on like the heathen, who imagine that the more they say the more likely they are to be heard. Do not imitate them, for your Father knows what your needs are before you ask him.

'This is how you should pray:

"Our Father in heaven,
may your name be hallowed;
your kingdom come,
your will be done,
on earth as in heaven.
Give us today our daily bread.
Forgive us the wrong we have done,
as we have forgiven those who have wronged us.
And do not put us to the test,
but save us from the evil one."

'For if you forgive others the wrongs they have done, your heavenly Father will also forgive you; but if you do not forgive others, then your Father will not forgive the wrongs that you have done.

'So too when you fast, do not look gloomy like the hypocrites: they make their faces unsightly so that everybody may see that they are fasting. Truly I tell you: they have their reward already. But when you fast, anoint your head and wash your face, so that no one sees that you are fasting, but only your Father who is in secret; and your Father who sees what is done in secret will give you your reward.

'Do not store up for yourselves treasure on earth, where moth and rust destroy, and thieves break in and steal; but store up treasure in heaven, where neither moth nor rust will destroy, nor thieves break in and steal. For where your treasure is, there will your heart be also.

'The lamp of the body is the eye. If your eyes are sound, you will have light for your whole body; if your eyes are bad, your whole body will be in darkness. If then the only light you have is darkness, how great a darkness that will be.

'No one can serve two masters; for either he will hate the first and love the second, or he will be devoted to the first and despise the second. You cannot serve God and Money.'

Do Not be Anxious

'This is why I tell you not to be anxious about food and drink to keep you alive and about clothes to cover your body. Surely life is more than food, the body more than clothes. Look at the birds in the sky; they do not sow and reap and store in barns, yet your heavenly Father feeds them. Are you not worth more than the birds? Can anxious thought add a single day to your life? And why be anxious about clothes? Consider how the lilies grow in the fields; they do not work, they do not spin; yet I tell you, even Solomon in all his splendour was not attired like one of them. If that is how God clothes the grass in the fields, which is there today and tomorrow is thrown on the stove, will he not all the more clothe you? How little faith you have! Do not ask anxiously, "What are we to eat? What are we to drink? What shall we wear?" These are the things that occupy the minds of the heathen, but your heavenly Father knows that you need them all. Set your mind on God's kingdom and his justice before everything else, and all the rest will come to you as well. So do not be anxious about tomorrow; tomorrow will look after itself. Each day has troubles enough of its own.'

Do Not Judge

'Do not judge, and you will not be judged. For as you judge others, so you will yourselves be judged, and whatever measure you deal out to others will be dealt to you. Why do you look at the speck of sawdust in your brother's eye, with never a thought for the plank in your own? How can you say to your brother, "Let me take the speck out of your eye," when all the time there is a plank in your own? You hypocrite! First take the plank out of your own eye, and then you will see clearly to take the speck out of your brother's.'

Concluding Teachings

'Do not give dogs what is holy; do not throw your pearls to the pigs: they will only trample on them, and turn and tear you to pieces.

'Ask, and you will receive; seek, and you will find; knock, and the door will be opened to you. For everyone who asks receives, those who seek find, and to those who knock, the door will be opened.

'Would any of you offer his son a stone when he asks for bread, or a snake when he asks for a fish? If you, bad as you are, know how to give good things to your children, how much more will your heavenly Father give good things to those who ask him!

'Always treat others as you would like them to treat you: that is the law and the prophets.

'Enter by the narrow gate. Wide is the gate and broad the road that leads to destruction, and many enter that way; narrow is the gate and constricted the road that leads to life, and those who find them are few.

'Beware of false prophets, who come to you dressed up as sheep while underneath they are savage wolves. You will recognize them by their fruit. Can grapes be picked from briars, or figs from thistles? A good tree always yields sound fruit, and a poor tree bad fruit. A good tree cannot bear bad fruit, or a poor tree sound fruit. A tree that does not yield sound fruit is cut down and thrown on the fire. That is why I say you will recognize them by their fruit.

'Not everyone who says to me, "Lord, Lord" will enter the kingdom of Heaven, but only those who do the will of my heavenly Father. When the day comes, many will say to me, "Lord, Lord, did we not prophesy in your name, drive out demons in your name, and in your name perform many miracles?" Then I will tell them plainly, "I never knew you. Out of my sight; your deeds are evil!"

'So whoever hears these words of mine and acts on them is like a man who had the sense to build his house on rock. The rain came down, the floods rose, the winds blew and beat upon that house; but it did not fall, because its foundations were on rock. And whoever hears these words of mine and does not act on them is like a man who was foolish enough to build his house on sand.

The rain came down, the floods rose, the winds blew and battered against that house; and it fell with a great crash.'

When Jesus had finished this discourse the people were amazed at his teaching; unlike their scribes he taught with a note of authority.

4 | HEALINGS AND TEACHINGS

Jesus Commissions the Twelve Disciples

Then he called his twelve disciples to him and gave them the following instructions: 'Do not take the road to gentile lands, and do not enter any Samaritan town; but go rather to the lost sheep of the house of Israel. And as you go proclaim the message: "The kingdom of Heaven is upon you." Heal the sick, raise the dead, cleanse lepers, drive out demons. You received without cost; give without charge.

'Take no gold, silver, or copper in your belts, no pack for the road, no second coat, no sandals, no stick; the worker deserves his keep.

'Whatever town or village you enter, look for some suitable person in it, and stay with him until you leave. Wish the house peace as you enter it; if it is welcoming, let your peace descend on it, and if it is not, let your peace come back to you. If anyone will not receive you or listen to what you say, then as you leave that house or that town shake the dust of it off your feet. Truly I tell you: on the day of judgement it will be more bearable for the land of Sodom and Gomorrah than for that town.

'I send you out like sheep among wolves; be wary as serpents, innocent as doves.

'Be on your guard, for you will be handed over to the courts, they will flog you in their synagogues, and you will be brought before governors and kings on my account, to testify before them and the Gentiles. But when you are arrested, do not worry about what you are to say, for when the time comes, the words you need will be given you; it will not be you speaking, but the Spirit of your Father speaking in you.

'Brother will hand over brother to death, and a father his child; children will turn against their parents and send them to their death. Everyone will hate you for your allegiance to me, but whoever endures to the end will be saved. When you are persecuted in one town, take refuge in another; truly I tell you: before you have gone through all the towns of Israel the Son of Man will have come.

'No pupil ranks above his teacher, no servant above his master. The pupil should be content to share his teacher's lot, the servant to share his master's. If the master has been called Beelzebul, how much more his household!

'So do not be afraid of them. There is nothing covered up that will not be uncovered, nothing hidden that will not be made known. What I say to you in the dark you must repeat in broad daylight; what you hear whispered you must shout from the housetops. Do not fear those who kill the body, but cannot kill the soul. Fear him rather who is able to destroy both soul and body in hell.

'Are not two sparrows sold for a penny? Yet without your Father's knowledge not one of them can fall to the ground. As for you, even the hairs of your head have all been counted. So do not be afraid; you are worth more than any number of sparrows.

'Whoever will acknowledge me before others, I will acknowledge before my Father in heaven; and whoever disowns me before others, I will disown before my Father in heaven.

'You must not think that I have come to bring peace to the earth; I have not come to bring peace, but a sword. I have come to set a man against his father, a daughter against her mother, a daughter-in-law against her mother-in-law; and a man will find his enemies under his own roof.

'No one is worthy of me who cares more for father or mother than for me; no one is worthy of me who cares more for son or daughter; no one is worthy of me who does not take up his cross and follow me. Whoever gains his life will lose it; whoever loses his life for my sake will gain it.

'To receive you is to receive me, and to receive me is to receive the One who sent me. Whoever receives a prophet because he is a prophet will be given a prophet's reward, and whoever receives a good man because he is a good man will be given a good man's reward. Truly I tell you: anyone who gives so much as a cup of cold water to one of these little ones because he is a disciple of mine, will certainly not go unrewarded.'

Jesus Teaches in Nearby Towns
Then he spoke of the towns in which most of his miracles had been performed, and denounced them for their impenitence. 'Alas for you, Chorazin!' he said. 'Alas for you, Bethsaida! If the miracles performed in you had taken place in Tyre and Sidon, they would have repented long ago in sackcloth and ashes. But it will be more bearable, I tell you, for Tyre and Sidon on the day of judgement than for you. As for you, Capernaum, will you be exalted to heaven? No, you will be brought down to Hades! For if the miracles performed in you had taken place in Sodom, Sodom would be standing to this day. But it will be more bearable, I tell you, for the land of Sodom on the day of judgement than for you.'

At that time Jesus spoke these words: 'I thank you, Father, Lord of heaven and earth, for hiding these things from the learned and wise, and revealing them to the simple. Yes, Father, such was your choice. Everything is entrusted to me by my Father; and no one knows the Son but the Father, and no one knows the Father but the Son and those to whom the Son chooses to reveal him.

'Come to me, all who are weary and whose load is heavy; I will give you rest. Take my yoke upon you, and learn from me, for I am gentle and humble-hearted; and you will find rest for your souls. For my yoke is easy to wear, my load is light.'

Jesus Commends John the Baptist
When John was informed of all this by his disciples, he summoned two of them and sent them to the Lord with this question:

'Are you the one who is to come, or are we to expect someone else?' The men made their way to Jesus and said, 'John the Baptist has sent us to ask you, "Are you the one who is to come, or are we to expect someone else?"' There and then he healed many sufferers from diseases, plagues, and evil spirits; and on many blind people he bestowed sight. Then he gave them this answer: 'Go and tell John what you have seen and heard: the blind regain their sight, the lame walk, lepers are made clean, the deaf hear, the dead are raised to life, the poor are brought good news and happy is he who does not find me an obstacle to faith.'

After John's messengers had left, Jesus began to speak about him to the crowds: 'What did you go out into the wilderness to see? A reed swaying in the wind? No? Then what did you go out to see? A man dressed in finery? Grand clothes and luxury are to be found in palaces. But what did you go out to see? A prophet? Yes indeed, and far more than a prophet. He is the man of whom scripture says,

"Here is my herald, whom I send ahead of you,
and he will prepare your way before you."

'I tell you, among all who have been born, no one has been greater than John; yet the least in the kingdom of God is greater than he is.' When they heard him, all the people, including the tax-collectors, acknowledged the goodness of God, for they had accepted John's baptism; but the Pharisees and lawyers, who had refused his baptism, rejected God's purpose for themselves.

'How can I describe the people of this generation? What are they like? They are like children sitting in the market-place and calling to each other,

"We piped for you and you would not dance.
We lamented, and you would not mourn."

'For John the Baptist came, neither eating bread nor drinking wine, and you say, "He is possessed." The Son of Man came, eating and drinking, and you say, "Look at him! A glutton and a drinker, a friend of tax-collectors and sinners!" And yet God's wisdom is proved right by all who are her children.'

A Woman Anoints Jesus's Feet

One of the Pharisees invited Jesus to a meal; he went to the Pharisee's house and took his place at table. A woman who was living an immoral life in the town had learned that Jesus was a guest in the Pharisee's house and had brought oil of myrrh in a small flask. She took her place behind him, by his feet, weeping. His feet were wet with her tears and she wiped them with her hair, kissing them and anointing them with the myrrh. When his host the Pharisee saw this he said to himself, 'If this man were a real prophet, he would know who this woman is who is touching him, and what a bad character she is.' Jesus took him up: 'Simon,' he said, 'I have something to say to you.' 'What is it, Teacher?' he asked. 'Two men were in debt to a moneylender: one owed him five hundred silver pieces, the other fifty. As they did not have the means to pay he cancelled both debts. Now, which will love him more?' Simon replied, 'I should think the one that was let off more.' 'You are right,' said Jesus. Then turning to the woman, he said to Simon, 'You see this woman? I came to your house: you provided no water for my feet; but this woman has made my feet wet with her tears and wiped them with her hair. You gave me no kiss; but she has been kissing my feet ever since I came in. You did not anoint my head with oil; but she has anointed my feet with myrrh. So, I tell you, her great love proves that her many sins have been forgiven; where little has been forgiven, little love is shown.' Then he said to her, 'Your sins are forgiven.' The other guests began to ask themselves, 'Who is this, that he can forgive sins?' But he said to the woman, 'Your faith has saved you; go in peace.'

The Women who Followed Jesus

After this he went journeying from town to town and village to village, proclaiming the good news of the kingdom of God. With him were the Twelve and a number of women who had been set free from evil spirits and infirmities: Mary, known as Mary of Magdala, from whom seven demons had come out, Joanna, the wife of Chuza a steward of Herod's, Susanna, and many others. These women provided for them out of their own resources.

Jesus Denounces the Pharisees

Then they brought him a man who was possessed by a demon; he was blind and dumb, and Jesus cured him, restoring both speech and sight. The bystanders were all amazed, and the word went round: 'Can this be the Son of David?' But when the Pharisees heard it they said, 'It is only by Beelzebul prince of devils that this man drives the devils out.'

Knowing what was in their minds, he said to them, 'Every kingdom divided against itself is laid waste; and no town or household that is divided against itself can stand. And if it is Satan who drives out Satan, he is divided against himself; how then can his kingdom stand? If it is by Beelzebul that I drive out devils, by whom do your own people drive them out? If this is your argument, they themselves will refute you. But if it is by the Spirit of God that I drive out the devils, then be sure the kingdom of God has already come upon you.

'Or again, how can anyone break into a strong man's house and make off with his goods, unless he has first tied up the strong man? Then he can ransack the house.

'He who is not with me is against me, and he who does not gather with me scatters.

'So I tell you this: every sin and every slander can be forgiven, except slander spoken against the Spirit; that will not be forgiven. Anyone who speaks a word against the Son of Man will be forgiven; but if anyone speaks against the Holy Spirit, for him there will be no forgiveness, either in this age or in the age to come.

'Get a good tree and its fruit will be good; get a bad tree and its fruit will be bad. You can tell a tree by its fruit. Vipers' brood! How can your words be good when you yourselves are evil? It is from the fullness of the heart that the mouth speaks. Good people from their store of good produce good; and evil people from their store of evil produce evil.

'I tell you this: every thoughtless word you speak you will have to account for on the day of judgement. For out of your own mouth you will be acquitted; out of your own mouth you will be condemned.'

At this some of the scribes and the Pharisees said, 'Teacher, we would like you to show us a sign.' He answered: 'It is a wicked, godless generation that asks for a sign, and the only sign that will be given it is the sign of the prophet Jonah. Just as Jonah was in the sea monster's belly for three days and three nights, so the Son of Man will be three days and three nights in the bowels of the earth. The men of Nineveh will appear in court when this generation is on trial, and ensure its condemnation, for they repented at the preaching of Jonah; and what is here is greater than Jonah. The queen of the south will appear in court when this generation is on trial, and ensure its condemnation; for she came from the ends of the earth to listen to the wisdom of Solomon, and what is here is greater than Solomon.

'When an unclean spirit comes out of someone it wanders over the desert sands seeking a resting-place, and finds none. Then it says, "I will go back to the home I left." So it returns and finds the house unoccupied, swept clean, and tidy. It goes off and collects seven other spirits more wicked than itself, and they all come in and settle there; and in the end that person's plight is worse than before. That is how it will be with this wicked generation.'

Brothers of Jesus
He was still speaking to the crowd when his mother and brothers appeared; they stood outside, wanting to speak to him. Someone said, 'Your mother and your brothers are standing outside; they

want to speak to you.' Jesus turned to the man who brought the message, and said, 'Who is my mother? Who are my brothers?' and pointing to his disciples, he said, 'Here are my mother and my brothers. Whoever does the will of my heavenly Father is my brother and sister and mother.'

The Parable of the Wheat and the Darnel

Here is another parable he gave them: 'The kingdom of Heaven is like this. A man sowed his field with good seed; but while everyone was asleep his enemy came, sowed darnel among the wheat, and made off. When the corn sprouted and began to fill out, the darnel could be seen among it. The farmer's men went to their master and said, "Sir, was it not good seed that you sowed in your field? So where has the darnel come from?" "This is an enemy's doing," he replied. "Well then," they said, "shall we go and gather the darnel?" "No," he answered; "in gathering it you might pull up the wheat at the same time. Let them both grow together till harvest; and at harvest time I will tell the reapers, 'Gather the darnel first, and tie it in bundles for burning; then collect the wheat into my barn.'"'

Then he sent the people away, and went into the house, where his disciples came to him and said, 'Explain to us the parable of the darnel in the field.' He replied, 'The sower of the good seed is the Son of Man. The field is the world; the good seed stands for the children of the Kingdom, the darnel for the children of the evil one, and the enemy who sowed the darnel is the devil. The harvest is the end of time, and the reapers are angels. As the darnel is gathered up and burnt, so at the end of time the Son of Man will send his angels, who will gather out of his kingdom every cause of sin, and all whose deeds are evil; these will be thrown into the blazing furnace, where there will be wailing and grinding of teeth. Then the righteous will shine like the sun in the kingdom of their Father. If you have ears, then hear.'

More Parables of the Kingdom
'The kingdom of Heaven is like yeast, which a woman took and mixed with three measures of flour till it was all leavened.'

'The kingdom of Heaven is like treasure which a man found buried in a field. He buried it again, and in joy went and sold everything he had, and bought the field.

'Again, the kingdom of Heaven is like this. A merchant looking out for fine pearls found one of very special value; so he went and sold everything he had and bought it.

'Again the kingdom of Heaven is like a net cast into the sea, where it caught fish of every kind. When it was full, it was hauled ashore. Then the men sat down and collected the good fish into baskets and threw the worthless away. That is how it will be at the end of time. The angels will go out, and they will separate the wicked from the good, and throw them into the blazing furnace, where there will be wailing and grinding of teeth.

'Have you understood all this?' he asked; and they answered, 'Yes.' So he said to them, 'When, therefore, a teacher of the law has become a learner in the kingdom of Heaven, he is like a householder who can produce from his store things new and old.'

The Beheading of John the Baptist
Now King Herod heard of Jesus, for his fame had spread, and people were saying, 'John the Baptist has been raised from the dead, and that is why these miraculous powers are at work in him.' Others said, 'It is Elijah.' Others again, 'He is a prophet like one of the prophets of old.' But when Herod heard of it, he said, 'This is John, whom I beheaded, raised from the dead.'

It was this Herod who had sent men to arrest John and put him in prison at the instance of his brother Philip's wife, Herodias, whom he had married. John had told him, 'You have no right to take your brother's wife.' Herodias nursed a grudge against John and would willingly have killed him, but she could not, for Herod went in awe of him, knowing him to be a good and holy man; so he gave him his protection. He liked to listen to him, although what he heard left him greatly disturbed.

Herodias found her opportunity when Herod on his birthday gave a banquet to his chief officials and commanders and the leading men of Galilee. Her daughter came in and danced, and so delighted Herod and his guests that the king said to the girl, 'Ask me for anything you like and I will give it to you.' He even said on oath: 'Whatever you ask I will give you, up to half my kingdom.' She went out and said to her mother, 'What shall I ask for?' She replied, 'The head of John the Baptist.' The girl hurried straight back to the king with her request: 'I want you to give me, here and now, on a dish, the head of John the Baptist.' The king was greatly distressed, yet because of his oath and his guests he could not bring himself to refuse her. He sent a soldier of the guard with orders to bring John's head; and the soldier went to the prison and beheaded him; then he brought the head on a dish, and gave it to the girl; and she gave it to her mother.

When John's disciples heard the news, they came and took his body away and laid it in a tomb.

The Healing at the Pool of Bethesda
Some time later, Jesus went up to Jerusalem for one of the Jewish festivals. Now at the Sheep Gate in Jerusalem there is a pool whose Hebrew name is Bethesda. It has five colonnades and in them lay a great number of sick people, blind, lame, and paralysed. Among them was a man who had been crippled for thirty-eight years. Jesus saw him lying there, and knowing that he had been ill a long time he asked him, 'Do you want to get well?' 'Sir,' he replied, 'I have no one to put me in the pool when the water is disturbed; while I am getting there, someone else steps into the pool before me.' Jesus answered, 'Stand up, take your bed and walk.' The man recovered instantly; he took up his bed, and began to walk.

That day was a sabbath. So the Jews said to the man who had been cured, 'It is the sabbath. It is against the law for you to carry your bed.' He answered, 'The man who cured me, he told me, "Take up your bed and walk."' They asked him, 'Who is this man who told you to take it up and walk?' But the man who had been cured did not know who it was; for the place was crowded and Jesus had slipped away. A little later Jesus found him in the temple and said to him, 'Now that you are well, give up your sinful ways, or something worse may happen to you.' The man went off and told the Jews that it was Jesus who had cured him.

It was for doing such things on the sabbath that the Jews began to take action against Jesus. He defended himself by saying, 'My Father continues to work, and I must work too.' This made the Jews all the more determined to kill him, because not only was he breaking the sabbath but, by calling God his own Father, he was claiming equality with God.

To this charge Jesus replied, 'In very truth I tell you, the Son can do nothing by himself; he does only what he sees the Father doing: whatever the Father does, the Son does. For the Father loves the Son and shows him all that he himself is doing, and will show him even greater deeds, to fill you with wonder. As the Father raises the dead and gives them life, so the Son gives life as he chooses. Again, the Father does not judge anyone, but has given full jurisdiction to the Son; it is his will that all should pay the same honour to the Son as to the Father. To deny honour to the Son is to deny it to the Father who sent him. You study the scriptures diligently, supposing that in having them you have eternal life; their testimony points to me, yet you refuse to come to me to receive that life.

'I do not look to men for honour. But I know that with you it is different, for you have no love of God in you. I have come accredited by my Father, and you have no welcome for me; but let someone self-accredited come, and you will give him a welcome. How can you believe when you accept honour from one another, and care nothing for the honour that comes from him who alone is God? Do not imagine that I shall be your accuser at the Father's tribunal. Your accuser is Moses, the very Moses on whom you have set your hope. If you believed him you would believe me, for it was of me that he wrote. But if you do not believe what he wrote, how are you to believe what I say?'

The Feeding of the Five Thousand
Some time later Jesus withdrew to the farther shore of the sea of Galilee (or Tiberias), and a large crowd of people followed him because they had seen the signs he performed in healing the sick. Jesus went up the hillside and sat down with his disciples. It was near the time of Passover, the great Jewish festival. Looking up and seeing a large crowd coming towards him, Jesus said to Philip, 'Where are we to buy bread to feed these people?' He said this to test him; Jesus himself knew what he meant to do. Philip replied, 'We would need two hundred denarii to buy enough bread for each of them to have a little.' One of his disciples, Andrew, the brother of Simon Peter, said to him, 'There is a boy here who has five barley loaves and two fish; but what is that among so many?' Jesus said, 'Make the people sit down.' There was plenty of grass there, so the men sat down, about five thousand of them. Then Jesus took the loaves, gave thanks, and distributed them to the people as they sat there. He did the same with the fish, and they had as much as they wanted. When everyone had had enough, he said to his disciples, 'Gather up the pieces left over, so that nothing is wasted.' They gathered them up, and filled twelve baskets with the pieces of the five barley loaves that were left uneaten.

Jesus Walks on the Water
As soon as they had finished, he made the disciples embark and cross to the other side ahead of him, while he dismissed the crowd; then he went up the hill by himself to pray. It had grown late, and he was there alone. The boat was already some distance from the shore, battling with a head wind and a rough sea. Between three and six in the morning he came towards them, walking across the lake. When the disciples saw him walking on

the lake they were so shaken that they cried out in terror: 'It is a ghost!' But at once Jesus spoke to them: 'Take heart! It is I; do not be afraid.'

Peter called to him: 'Lord, if it is you, tell me to come to you over the water.' 'Come,' said Jesus. Peter got down out of the boat, and walked over the water towards Jesus. But when he saw the strength of the gale he was afraid; and beginning to sink, he cried, 'Save me, Lord!' Jesus at once reached out and caught hold of him. 'Why did you hesitate?' he said. 'How little faith you have!' Then they climbed into the boat; and the wind dropped. And the men in the boat fell at his feet, exclaiming, 'You must be the Son of God.'

The Bread of Life
Next morning the crowd was still on the opposite shore. They had seen only one boat there, and Jesus, they knew, had not embarked with his disciples, who had set off by themselves. Boats from Tiberias, however, had come ashore near the place where the people had eaten the bread over which the Lord gave thanks. When the crowd saw that Jesus had gone as well as his disciples, they went on board these boats and made for Capernaum in search of him. They found him on the other side. 'Rabbi,' they asked, 'when did you come here?' Jesus replied, 'In very truth I tell you, it is not because you saw signs that you came looking for me, but because you ate the bread and your hunger was satisfied. You should work, not for this perishable food, but for the food that lasts, the food of eternal life. This food the Son of Man will give you, for on him God the Father has set the seal of his authority.' 'Then what must we do', they asked him, 'if our work is to be the work of God?' Jesus replied, 'This is the work that God requires: to believe in the one whom he has sent.'

They asked, 'What sign can you give us, so that we may see it and believe you? What is the work you are doing? Our ancestors had manna to eat in the desert; as scripture says, "He gave them bread from heaven to eat."' Jesus answered, 'In very truth I tell you, it was not Moses who gave you the bread from heaven; it is my Father who gives you the true bread from heaven. The bread that God gives comes down from heaven and brings life to the world.' 'Sir,' they said to him, 'give us this bread now and always.' Jesus said to them, 'I am the bread of life. Whoever comes to me will never be hungry, and whoever believes in me will never be thirsty. But you, as I said, have seen and yet you do not believe. All that the Father gives me will come to me, and anyone who comes to me I will never turn away. I am the living bread that has come down from heaven; if anyone eats this bread, he will live for ever. The bread which I shall give is my own flesh, given for the life of the world.'

This led to a fierce dispute among the Jews. 'How can this man give us his flesh to eat?' they protested. Jesus answered them, 'In very truth I tell you, unless you eat the flesh of the Son of Man and drink his blood you can have no life in you. Whoever eats my flesh and drinks my blood has eternal life, and I will raise him up on the last day. My flesh is real food; my blood is real drink. Whoever eats my flesh and drinks my blood dwells in me and I in him.'

The Meaning of Defilement
A group of Pharisees, with some scribes who had come from Jerusalem, met him and noticed that some of his disciples were eating their food with defiled hands – in other words, without washing them. (For Pharisees and Jews in general never eat without washing their hands, in obedience to ancient tradition; and on coming from the market-place they never eat without first washing. And there are many other points on which they maintain traditional rules, for example in the washing of cups and jugs and copper bowls.) These Pharisees and scribes questioned Jesus: 'Why do your disciples not conform to the ancient tradition, but eat their food with defiled hands?' He answered, 'How right Isaiah was when he prophesied about you hypocrites in these words: "This people pays me lip-service, but their heart is far from me: they worship me in vain, for they teach as doctrines the

commandments of men." You neglect the commandment of God, in order to maintain the tradition of men.'

He said to them, 'How clever you are at setting aside the commandment of God in order to maintain your tradition! Moses said, "Honour your father and your mother," and again, "Whoever curses his father or mother shall be put to death." But you hold that if someone says to his father or mother, "Anything I have which might have been used for your benefit is Corban,"' (that is, set apart for God) 'he is no longer allowed to do anything for his father or mother. In this way by your tradition, handed down among you, you make God's word null and void. And you do many other things just like that.'

On another occasion he called the people and said to them, 'Listen to me, all of you, and understand this: nothing that goes into a person from outside can defile him; no, it is the things that come out of a person that defile him.'

When he had left the people and gone indoors, his disciples questioned him about the parable. He said to them, 'Are you as dull as the rest? Do you not see that nothing that goes into a person from outside can defile him, because it does not go into the heart but into the stomach, and so goes out into the drain?' By saying this he declared all foods clean. He went on, 'It is what comes out of a person that defiles him. From inside, from the human heart, come evil thoughts, acts of fornication, theft, murder, adultery, greed, and malice; fraud, indecency, envy, slander, arrogance, and folly; all these evil things come from within, and they are what defile a person.'

Jesus and the Syro-Phoenician Woman

He moved on from there into the territory of Tyre. He found a house to stay in, and would have liked to remain unrecognized, but that was impossible. Almost at once a woman whose small daughter was possessed by an unclean spirit heard of him and came and fell at his feet. (The woman was a Gentile, a Phoenician of Syria by nationality.) She begged him to drive the demon out of her daughter. He said to her, 'Let the children be satisfied first; it is not right to take the children's bread and throw it to the dogs.' 'Sir,' she replied, 'even the dogs under the table eat the children's scraps.' He said to her, 'For saying that, go, and you will find the demon has left your daughter.' And when she returned home, she found the child lying in bed; the demon had left her.

The Healing of a Deaf Man

On his journey back from Tyrian territory he went by way of Sidon to the sea of Galilee, well within the territory of the Decapolis. They brought to him a man who was deaf and had an impediment in his speech, and begged Jesus to lay his hand on him. He took him aside, away from the crowd; then he put his fingers in the man's ears, and touched his tongue with spittle. Looking up to heaven, he sighed, and said to him, '*Ephphatha*,' which means 'Be opened.' With that his hearing was restored, and at the same time the impediment was removed and he spoke clearly. Jesus forbade them to tell anyone; but the more he forbade them, the more they spread it abroad. Their astonishment knew no bounds: 'All that he does, he does well,' they said; 'he even makes the deaf hear and the dumb speak.'

The Healing of a Blind Man

They arrived at Bethsaida. There the people brought a blind man to Jesus and begged him to touch him. He took the blind man by the hand and led him out of the village. Then he spat on his eyes, laid his hands upon him, and asked whether he could see anything. The man's sight began to come back, and he said, 'I see people – they look like trees, but they are walking about.' Jesus laid his hands on his eyes again; he looked hard, and now he was cured and could see everything clearly. Then Jesus sent him home, saying, 'Do not even go into the village.'

Peter's Confession

When he came to the territory of Caesarea Philippi, Jesus asked his disciples, 'Who do people say that the Son of Man is?' They answered, 'Some say John the Baptist, others Elijah, others Jeremiah, or one of the prophets.' 'And you,' he asked, 'who do you say I am?' Simon Peter answered: 'You are the Messiah, the Son of the living God.' Then Jesus said: 'Simon son of Jonah, you are favoured indeed! You did not learn that from any human being; it was revealed to you by my heavenly Father. And I say to you: you are Peter, the Rock; and on this rock I will build my church, and the powers of death shall never conquer it. I will give you the keys of the kingdom of Heaven; what you forbid on earth shall be forbidden in heaven, and what you allow on earth shall be allowed in heaven.' He then gave his disciples strict orders not to tell anyone that he was the Messiah.

Jesus Foretells his Passion

From that time Jesus began to make it clear to his disciples that he had to go to Jerusalem, and endure great suffering at the hands of the elders, chief priests, and scribes; to be put to death, and to be raised again on the third day. At this Peter took hold of him and began to rebuke him: 'Heaven forbid!' he said. 'No, Lord, this shall never happen to you.' Then Jesus turned and said to Peter, 'Out of my sight, Satan; you are a stumbling block to me. You think as men think, not as God thinks.'

Jesus then said to his disciples, 'Anyone who wishes to be a follower of mine must renounce self; he must take up his cross and follow me. Whoever wants to save his life will lose it, but whoever loses his life for my sake will find it. What will anyone gain by winning the whole world at the cost of his life? Or what can he give to buy his life back? For the Son of Man is to come in the glory of his Father with his angels, and then he will give everyone his due reward. Truly I tell you: there are some of those standing here who will not taste death before they have seen the Son of Man coming in his kingdom.'

The Transfiguration

Six days later Jesus took Peter, James, and John with him and led them up a high mountain by themselves. And in their presence he was transfigured; his clothes became dazzling white, with a whiteness no bleacher on earth could equal. They saw Elijah appear and Moses with him, talking with Jesus. Then Peter spoke: 'Rabbi,' he said, 'it is good that we are here! Shall we make three shelters, one for you, one for Moses, and one for Elijah?' For he did not know what to say; they were so terrified. Then a cloud appeared, casting its shadow over them, and out of the cloud came a voice: 'This is my beloved Son; listen to him.' And suddenly, when they looked around, only Jesus was with them; there was no longer anyone else to be seen.

On their way down the mountain, he instructed them not to tell anyone what they had seen until the Son of Man had risen from the dead. They seized upon those words, and discussed among themselves what this 'rising from the dead' could mean. And they put a question to him: 'Why do the scribes say that Elijah must come first?' He replied, 'Elijah does come first to set everything right. How is it, then, that the scriptures say of the Son of Man that he is to endure great suffering and be treated with contempt? However, I tell you, Elijah has already come and they have done to him what they wanted, as the scriptures say of him.'

The Healing of a Boy Possessed by a Spirit

When they came back to the disciples they saw a large crowd surrounding them and scribes arguing with them. As soon as they saw Jesus the whole crowd were overcome with awe and ran forward to welcome him. He asked them, 'What is this argument about?' A man in the crowd spoke up: 'Teacher, I brought my son for you to cure. He is possessed by a spirit that makes him dumb. Whenever it attacks him, it flings him to the ground, and he foams at the mouth, grinds his teeth, and goes rigid. I asked your disciples to drive it out, but they could not.' Jesus answered: 'What an unbelieving generation! How long shall I be with you?

How long must I endure you? Bring him to me.' So they brought the boy to him; and as soon as the spirit saw him it threw the boy into convulsions, and he fell on the ground and rolled about foaming at the mouth. Jesus asked his father, 'How long has he been like this?' 'From childhood,' he replied; 'it has often tried to destroy him by throwing him into the fire or into water. But if it is at all possible for you, take pity on us and help us.' 'If it is possible!' said Jesus. 'Everything is possible to one who believes.' At once the boy's father cried: 'I believe; help my unbelief.' When Jesus saw that the crowd was closing in on them, he spoke sternly to the unclean spirit. 'Deaf and dumb spirit,' he said, 'I command you, come out of him and never go back!' It shrieked aloud and threw the boy into repeated convulsions, and then came out, leaving him looking like a corpse; in fact, many said, 'He is dead.' But Jesus took hold of his hand and raised him to his feet, and he stood up.

Then Jesus went indoors, and his disciples asked him privately, 'Why could we not drive it out?' He said, 'This kind cannot be driven out except by prayer.'

Paying the Temple Tax

On their arrival at Capernaum the collectors of the temple tax came up to Peter and asked, 'Does your master not pay temple tax?' 'He does,' said Peter. When he went indoors Jesus forestalled him by asking, 'Tell me, Simon, from whom do earthly monarchs collect tribute money? From their own people, or from aliens?' 'From aliens,' said Peter. 'Yes,' said Jesus, 'and their own people are exempt. But as we do not want to cause offence, go and cast a line in the lake; take the first fish you catch, open its mouth, and you will find a silver coin; take that and pay the tax for us both.'

The Greatest in the Kingdom

At that time the disciples came to Jesus and asked, 'Who is the greatest in the kingdom of Heaven?' He called a child, set him in front of them, and said, 'Truly I tell you: unless you turn round and become like children, you will never enter the kingdom of Heaven. Whoever humbles himself and becomes like this child will be the greatest in the kingdom of Heaven, and whoever receives one such child in my name receives me. But if anyone causes the downfall of one of these little ones who believe in me, it would be better for him to have a millstone hung round his neck and be drowned in the depths of the sea. Alas for the world that any of them should be made to fall! Such things must happen, but alas for the one through whom they happen!'

Reproof and Reconciliation

'If your brother does wrong, go and take the matter up with him, strictly between yourselves. If he listens to you, you have won your brother over. But if he will not listen, take one or two others with you, so that every case may be settled on the evidence of two or three witnesses. If he refuses to listen to them, report the matter to the congregation; and if he will not listen even to the congregation, then treat him as you would a pagan or a tax-collector.

'Truly I tell you: whatever you forbid on earth shall be forbidden in heaven, and whatever you allow on earth shall be allowed in heaven.

'And again I tell you: if two of you agree on earth about any request you have to make, that request will be granted by my heavenly Father. For where two or three meet together in my name, I am there among them.'

Then Peter came to him and asked, 'Lord, how often am I to forgive my brother if he goes on wronging me? As many as seven times?' Jesus replied, 'I do not say seven times but seventy times seven.'

The Parable of the Unmerciful Servant

'The kingdom of Heaven, therefore, should be thought of in this way: There was once a king who decided to settle accounts with the men who served him. At the outset there appeared before him a man who owed ten thousand talents. Since he had no means of paying, his master ordered him to be sold, with his wife, his children, and everything he had, to meet the debt. The man fell at his master's feet. "Be patient with me," he implored, "and I will pay you in full"; and the master was so moved with pity that he let the man go and cancelled the debt. But no sooner had the man gone out than he met a fellow servant who owed him a hundred denarii; he took hold of him, seizing him by the throat, and said, "Pay me what you owe." The man fell at his fellow servant's feet, and begged him, "Be patient with me, and I will pay you"; but he refused, and had him thrown into jail until he should pay the debt. The other servants were deeply distressed when they saw what had happened, and they went to their master and told him the whole story. Then he sent for the man and said, "You scoundrel! I cancelled the whole of your debt when you appealed to me; ought you not to have shown mercy to your fellow servant just as I showed mercy to you?" And so angry was the master that he condemned the man to be tortured until he should pay the debt in full. That is how my heavenly Father will deal with you, unless you each forgive your brother from your hearts.'

Not One of Us
'Master,' said John, 'we saw someone driving out demons in your name, but as he is not one of us we tried to stop him.' Jesus said to him, 'Do not stop him, for he who is not against you is on your side.'

5 | THE ROAD TO JERUSALEM

No Looking Back

As the time approached when he was to be taken up to heaven, Jesus set his face resolutely towards Jerusalem.

As they were going along the road a man said to him, 'I will follow you wherever you go.' Jesus answered, 'Foxes have their holes and birds their roosts; but the Son of Man has nowhere to lay his head.' To another he said, 'Follow me,' but the man replied, 'Let me first go and bury my father.' Jesus said, 'Leave the dead to bury their dead; you must go and announce the kingdom of God.' Yet another said, 'I will follow you, sir; but let me first say goodbye to my people at home.' To him Jesus said, 'No one who sets his hand to the plough and then looks back is fit for the kingdom of God.'

Jesus Commissions More Disciples

After this the Lord appointed a further seventy-two and sent them on ahead in pairs to every town and place he himself intended to visit. He said to them: 'The crop is heavy, but the labourers are few. Ask the owner therefore to send labourers to bring in the harvest. Be on your way; I am sending you like lambs among wolves. Carry no purse or pack, and travel barefoot. Exchange no greetings on the road. When you go into a house, let your first words be, "Peace to this house." If there is a man of peace there, your peace will rest on him; if not, it will return to you. Stay in that house, sharing their food and drink; for the worker deserves his pay.'

The seventy-two came back jubilant. 'In your name, Lord,' they said, 'even the demons submit to us.' He replied, 'I saw

Satan fall, like lightning, from heaven. And I have given you the power to tread underfoot snakes and scorpions and all the forces of the enemy. Nothing will ever harm you. Nevertheless, do not rejoice that the spirits submit to you, but that your names are enrolled in heaven.'

When he was alone with his disciples he turned to them and said, 'Happy the eyes that see what you are seeing! I tell you, many prophets and kings wished to see what you now see, yet never saw it; to hear what you hear, yet never heard it.'

The Parable of the Good Samaritan

A lawyer once came forward to test him by asking: 'Teacher, what must I do to inherit eternal life?' Jesus said, 'What is written in the law? What is your reading of it?' He replied, 'Love the Lord your God with all your heart, and with all your soul, with all your strength, and with all your mind; and your neighbour as yourself.' 'That is the right answer,' said Jesus; 'do that and you will have life.'

Wanting to justify his question, he asked, 'But who is my neighbour?' Jesus replied, 'A man was on his way from Jerusalem down to Jericho when he was set upon by robbers, who stripped and beat him, and went off leaving him half dead. It so happened that a priest was going down by the same road, and when he saw him, he went past on the other side. So too a Levite came to the place, and when he saw him went past on the other side. But a Samaritan who was going that way came upon him, and when he saw him he was moved to pity. He went up and bandaged his wounds, bathing them with oil and wine. Then he lifted him on to his own beast, brought him to an inn, and looked after him. Next day he produced two silver pieces and gave them to the innkeeper, and said, "Look after him; and if you spend more, I will repay you on my way back." Which of these three do you think was neighbour to the man who fell into the hands of the robbers?' He answered, 'The one who showed him kindness.' Jesus said to him, 'Go and do as he did.'

In the House of Mary and Martha

While they were on their way Jesus came to a village where a woman named Martha made him welcome. She had a sister, Mary, who seated herself at the Lord's feet and stayed there listening to his words. Now Martha was distracted by her many tasks, so she came to him and said, 'Lord, do you not care that my sister has left me to get on with the work by myself? Tell her to come and give me a hand.' But the Lord answered, 'Martha, Martha, you are fretting and fussing about so many things; only one thing is necessary. Mary has chosen what is best; it shall not be taken away from her.'

The Parable of the Persistent Friend

Then he said to them, 'Suppose one of you has a friend who comes to him in the middle of the night and says, "My friend, lend me three loaves, for a friend of mine on a journey has turned up at my house, and I have nothing to offer him"; and he replies from inside, "Do not bother me. The door is shut for the night; my children and I have gone to bed; and I cannot get up and give you what you want." I tell you that even if he will not get up and provide for him out of friendship, his very persistence will make the man get up and give him all he needs.'

Warnings Against the Pharisees

When he had finished speaking, a Pharisee invited him to a meal, and he came in and sat down. The Pharisee noticed with surprise that he had not begun by washing before the meal. But the Lord said to him, 'You Pharisees clean the outside of cup and plate; but inside you are full of greed and wickedness. You fools! Did not he who made the outside make the inside too? But let what is inside be given in charity, and all is clean.

'Alas for you Pharisees! You pay tithes of mint and rue and every garden herb, but neglect justice and the love of God. It is these you should have practised, without overlooking the others.

'Alas for you Pharisees! You love to have the chief seats in synagogues, and to be greeted respectfully in the street.

'Alas, alas, you are like unmarked graves which people walk over unawares.'

At this one of the lawyers said, 'Teacher, when you say things like this you are insulting us too.' Jesus rejoined: 'Alas for you lawyers also! You load men with intolerable burdens, and will not lift a finger to lighten the load.

'Alas, you build monuments to the prophets whom your fathers murdered, and so testify that you approve of the deeds your fathers did; they committed the murders and you provide the monuments.

'This is why the Wisdom of God said, "I will send them prophets and messengers; and some of these they will persecute and kill"; so that this generation will have to answer for the blood of all the prophets shed since the foundation of the world; from the blood of Abel to the blood of Zechariah who met his death between the altar and the sanctuary. I tell you, this generation will have to answer for it all.

'Alas for you lawyers! You have taken away the key of knowledge. You did not go in yourselves, and those who were trying to go in, you prevented.'

After he had left the house, the scribes and Pharisees began to assail him fiercely and to ply him with a host of questions, laying snares to catch him with his own words.

The Parable of the Rich Fool

Someone in the crowd said to him, 'Teacher, tell my brother to divide the family property with me.' He said to the man, 'Who set me over you to judge or arbitrate?' Then to the people he said, 'Beware! Be on your guard against greed of every kind, for even when someone has more than enough, his possessions do not give him life.' And he told them this parable: 'There was a rich man whose land yielded a good harvest. He debated with himself: "What am I to do? I have not the space to store my produce. This is what I will do," said he: "I will pull down my barns and build them bigger. I will collect in them all my grain and other goods, and I will say to myself, 'You have plenty of good things laid by, enough for many years to come: take life easy, eat, drink, and enjoy yourself.'" But God said to him, "You fool, this very night you must surrender your life; and the money you have made, who will get it now?" That is how it is with the man who piles up treasure for himself and remains a pauper in the sight of God.'

The Need for Repentance

At that time some people came and told him about the Galileans whose blood Pilate had mixed with their sacrifices. He answered them: 'Do you suppose that, because these Galileans suffered this fate, they must have been greater sinners than anyone else in Galilee? No, I tell you; but unless you repent, you will all of you come to the same end. Or the eighteen people who were killed when the tower fell on them at Siloam – do you imagine they must have been more guilty than all the other people living in Jerusalem? No, I tell you; but unless you repent, you will all come to an end like theirs.'

The Parable of the Barren Fig Tree

He told them this parable: 'A man had a fig tree growing in his vineyard; and he came looking for fruit on it, but found none. So he said to the vine-dresser, "For the last three years I have come looking for fruit on this fig tree without finding any. Cut it down. Why should it go on taking goodness from the soil?" But he replied, "Leave it, sir, for this one year, while I dig round it and manure it. And if it bears next season, well and good; if not, you shall have it down."'

The Healing of a Crippled Woman

He was teaching in one of the synagogues on the sabbath, and there was a woman there possessed by a spirit that had crippled her for eighteen years. She was bent double and quite unable to stand up straight. When Jesus saw her he called her and said, 'You are rid of your trouble,' and he laid his hands on her. Immediately she straightened up and began to praise God. But the president of the synagogue, indignant with Jesus for healing on the sabbath, intervened and said to the congregation, 'There are six working days: come and be cured on one of them, and not on the sabbath.' The Lord gave him this answer: 'What hypocrites you are!' he said. 'Is there a single one of you who does not loose his ox or his donkey from its stall and take it out to water on the sabbath? And here is this woman, a daughter of Abraham, who has been bound by Satan for eighteen long years: was it not right for her to be loosed from her bonds on the sabbath?' At these words all his opponents were covered with confusion, while the mass of the people were delighted at all the wonderful things he was doing.

A Warning Against Herod

At that time a number of Pharisees came and warned him, 'Leave this place and be on your way; Herod wants to kill you.' He replied, 'Go and tell that fox, "Listen: today and tomorrow I shall be driving out demons and working cures; on the third day I reach my goal." However, I must go on my way today and tomorrow and the next day, because it is unthinkable for a prophet to meet his death anywhere but in Jerusalem.

'O Jerusalem, Jerusalem, city that murders the prophets and stones the messengers sent to her! How often have I longed to gather your children, as a hen gathers her brood under her wings; but you would not let me. Look! There is your temple, forsaken by God. I tell you, you will not see me until the time comes when you say, "Blessings on him who comes in the name of the Lord!"'

The Healing of a Man with Dropsy

One sabbath he went to have a meal in the house of one of the leading Pharisees; and they were watching him closely. There, in front of him, was a man suffering from dropsy, and Jesus asked the lawyers and the Pharisees: 'Is it permitted to heal people on the sabbath or not?' They said nothing. So he took the man, cured him, and sent him away.

The Need for Humility

When he noticed how the guests were trying to secure the places of honour, he spoke to them in a parable: 'When somebody asks you to a wedding feast, do not sit down in the place of honour. It may be that some person more distinguished than yourself has been invited; and the host will come to say to you, "Give this man your seat." Then you will look foolish as you go to take the lowest place. No, when you receive an invitation, go and sit down in the lowest place, so that when your host comes he will say, "Come up higher, my friend." Then all your fellow guests will see the respect in which you are held. For everyone who exalts himself will be humbled; and whoever humbles himself will be exalted.'

Then he said to his host, 'When you are having guests for lunch or supper, do not invite your friends, your brothers or other relations, or your rich neighbours; they will only ask you back again and so you will be repaid. But when you give a party, ask the poor, the crippled, the lame, and the blind. That is the way to find happiness, because they have no means of repaying you. You will be repaid on the day when the righteous rise from the dead.'

The Parable of the Great Banquet

Hearing this, one of the company said to him, 'Happy are those who will sit at the feast in the kingdom of God!' Jesus answered, 'A man was giving a big dinner party and had sent out many invitations. At dinner-time he sent his servant to tell his guests, "Come please, everything is now ready." One after another they all sent excuses. The first said, "I have bought a piece of land, and I must go and inspect it; please accept my apologies." The second said, "I have bought five yoke of oxen, and I am on my way to try them out; please accept my apologies." The next said, "I cannot come; I have just got married." When the servant came back he reported this to his master. The master of the house was furious and said to him, "Go out quickly into the streets and alleys of the town, and bring in the poor, the crippled, the blind, and the lame." When the servant informed him that his orders had been carried out and there was still room, his master replied, "Go out on the highways and along the hedgerows and compel them to come in; I want my house full. I tell you, not one of those who were invited shall taste my banquet."'

The Cost of Discipleship

Once when great crowds were accompanying him, he turned to them and said: 'If anyone comes to me and does not hate his father and mother, wife and children, brothers and sisters, even his own life, he cannot be a disciple of mine. No one who does not carry his cross and come with me can be a disciple of mine. Would any of you think of building a tower without first sitting down and calculating the cost, to see whether he could afford to finish it? Otherwise, if he has laid its foundation and then is unable to complete it, everyone who sees it will laugh at him. "There goes the man", they will say, "who started to build and could not finish." Or what king will march to battle against another king, without first sitting down to consider whether with ten thousand men he can face an enemy coming to meet him with twenty thousand? If he cannot, then, long before the enemy approaches, he sends envoys and asks for terms. So also, if you are not prepared to leave all your possessions behind, you cannot be my disciples.

The Parable of the Lost Sheep

Another time, the tax-collectors and sinners were all crowding in to listen to him; and the Pharisees and scribes began murmuring their disapproval: 'This fellow', they said, 'welcomes sinners and eats with them.' He answered them with this parable: 'If one of you has a hundred sheep and loses one of them, does he not leave the ninety-nine in the wilderness and go after the one that is missing until he finds it? And when he does, he lifts it joyfully on to his shoulders, and goes home to call his friends and neighbours together. "Rejoice with me!" he cries. "I have found my lost sheep." In the same way, I tell you, there will be greater joy in heaven over one sinner who repents than over ninety-nine righteous people who do not need to repent.

The Parable of the Lost Coin

'Or again, if a woman has ten silver coins and loses one of them, does she not light the lamp, sweep out the house, and look in every corner till she finds it? And when she does, she calls her friends and neighbours together, and says, "Rejoice with me! I have found the coin that I lost." In the same way, I tell you, there is joy among the angels of God over one sinner who repents.'

The Parable of the Prodigal Son

Again he said: 'There was once a man who had two sons; and the younger said to his father, "Father, give me my share of the property." So he divided his estate between them. A few days later the younger son turned the whole of his share into cash and left home for a distant country, where he squandered it in dissolute living. He had spent it all, when a severe famine fell upon that country and he began to be in need. So he went and attached himself to one of the local landowners, who sent him on to his farm to mind the pigs. He would have been glad to fill his belly with the pods that the pigs were eating, but no one gave him anything. Then he came to his senses: "How many of my father's hired servants have more food than they can eat," he said, "and here am I, starving to death! I will go at once to my father, and say to him, 'Father, I have sinned against God and against you; I am no longer fit to be called your son; treat me as one of your hired servants.'" So he set out for his father's house. But while he was still a long way off his father saw him, and his heart went out to him; he ran to meet him, flung his arms round him, and kissed him. The son said, "Father, I have sinned against God and against you; I am no longer fit to be called your son." But the father said to his servants, "Quick! Fetch a robe, the best we have, and put it on him; put a ring on his finger and sandals on his feet. Bring the fatted calf and kill it, and let us celebrate with a feast. For this son of mine was dead and has come back to life; he was lost and is found." And the festivities began.

'Now the elder son had been out on the farm; and on his way back, as he approached the house, he heard music and dancing. He called one of the servants and asked what it meant. The servant told him, "Your brother has come home, and your father has killed the fatted calf because he has him back safe and sound." But he was angry and refused to go in. His father came out and pleaded with him; but he retorted, "You know how I have slaved for you all these years; I never once disobeyed your orders; yet you never gave me so much as a kid, to celebrate with my friends. But now that this son of yours turns up, after running through your money with his women, you kill the fatted calf for him." "My boy," said the father, "you are always with me, and everything I have is yours. How could we fail to celebrate this happy day? Your brother here was dead and has come back to life; he was lost and has been found."'

The Parable of the Unjust Steward

He said to his disciples, 'There was a rich man who had a steward, and he received complaints that this man was squandering the property. So he sent for him, and said, "What is this that I hear about you? Produce your accounts, for you cannot be steward any longer." The steward said to himself, "What am I to do now that my master is going to dismiss me from my post? I am not strong enough to dig, and I am too proud to beg. I know what I must do, to make sure that, when I am dismissed, there will be people who will take me into their homes." He summoned his master's debtors one by one. To the first he said, "How much do you owe my master?" He replied, "A hundred jars of olive oil." He said, "Here is your account. Sit down and make it fifty, and be quick about it." Then he said to another, "And you, how much do you owe?" He said, "A hundred measures of wheat," and was told, "Here is your account; make it eighty." And the master applauded the dishonest steward for acting so astutely. For in dealing with their own kind the children of this world are more astute than the children of light.

'So I say to you, use your worldly wealth to win friends for yourselves, so that when money is a thing of the past you may be received into an eternal home.'

On Divorce and Celibacy

Some Pharisees came and tested him by asking, 'Is it lawful for a man to divorce his wife for any cause he pleases?' He responded by asking, 'Have you never read that in the beginning the Creator made them male and female?' and he added, 'That is why a man leaves his father and mother, and is united to his wife, and the two become one flesh. It follows that they are no longer two individuals: they are one flesh. Therefore what God has joined together, man must not separate.' 'Then why', they objected, 'did Moses lay it down that a man might divorce his wife by a certificate of dismissal?' He answered, 'It was because of your stubbornness that Moses gave you permission to divorce your wives; but it was not like that at the beginning. I tell you, if a man divorces his wife for any cause other than unchastity, and marries another, he commits adultery.'

The disciples said to him, 'If that is how things stand for a man with a wife, it is better not to marry.' To this he replied, 'That is a course not everyone can accept, but only those for whom God has appointed it. For while some are incapable of marriage because they were born so, or were made so by men, there are others who have renounced marriage for the sake of the kingdom of Heaven. Let those accept who can.'

The Parable of the Rich Man and Lazarus

'There was once a rich man, who used to dress in purple and the finest linen, and feasted sumptuously every day. At his gate lay a poor man named Lazarus, who was covered with sores. He would have been glad to satisfy his hunger with the scraps from the rich man's table. Dogs used to come and lick his sores. One day the poor man died and was carried away by the angels to be with Abraham. The rich man also died and was buried. In Hades, where he was in torment, he looked up and there, far away, was Abraham with Lazarus close beside him. "Abraham, my father," he called out, "take pity on me! Send Lazarus to dip the tip of his finger in water, to cool my tongue, for I am in agony in this fire." But Abraham said, "My child, remember that the good things fell to you in your lifetime, and the bad to Lazarus. Now he has his consolation here and it is you who are in agony. But that is not all: there is a great gulf fixed between us; no one can cross it from our side to reach you, and none may pass from your side to us." "Then, father," he replied, "will you send him to my father's house, where I have five brothers, to warn them, so that they may not come to this place of torment?" But Abraham said, "They have Moses and the prophets; let them listen to them." "No, father Abraham," he replied, "but if someone from the dead visits them, they will repent." Abraham answered, "If they do not listen to Moses and the prophets they will pay no heed even if someone should rise from the dead."'

The Parable of the Dutiful Servants

'Suppose one of you has a servant ploughing or minding sheep. When he comes in from the fields, will the master say, "Come and sit down straight away"? Will he not rather say, "Prepare my supper; hitch up your robe, and wait on me while I have my meal. You can have yours afterwards"? Is he grateful to the servant for carrying out his orders? So with you: when you have carried out all you have been ordered to do, you should say, "We are servants and deserve no credit; we have only done our duty."'

The Cleansing of Ten Lepers

In the course of his journey to Jerusalem he was travelling through the borderlands of Samaria and Galilee. As he was entering a village he was met by ten men with leprosy. They stood some way off and called out to him, 'Jesus, Master, take pity on us.' When he saw them he said, 'Go and show yourselves to the priests'; and while they were on their way, they were made clean. One of them, finding himself cured, turned back with shouts of praise to God. He threw himself down at Jesus's feet and thanked him. And he was a Samaritan. At this Jesus said: 'Were not all ten made clean? The other nine, where are they? Was no one found returning to give praise to God except this foreigner?' And he said to the man, 'Stand up and go on your way; your faith has cured you.'

The Day of the Son of Man

The Pharisees asked him, 'When will the kingdom of God come?' He answered, 'You cannot tell by observation when the kingdom of God comes. You cannot say, "Look, here it is," or "There it is!" For the kingdom of God is among you!'

He said to the disciples, 'The time will come when you will long to see one of the days of the Son of Man and will not see it. They will say to you, "Look! There!" and "Look! Here!" Do not go running off in pursuit. For like a lightning-flash, that lights up the earth from end to end, will the Son of Man be in his day. But first he must endure much suffering and be rejected by this generation.

'As it was in the days of Noah, so will it be in the days of the Son of Man. They ate and drank and married, until the day that Noah went into the ark and the flood came and made an end of them all. So too in the days of Lot, they ate and drank, they bought and sold, they planted and built; but on the day that Lot left Sodom, fire and sulphur rained from the sky and made an end of them all. It will be like that on the day when the Son of Man is revealed.

'On that day if anyone is on the roof while his belongings are in the house, he must not go down to fetch them; and if anyone is in the field, he must not turn back. Remember Lot's wife. Whoever seeks to preserve his life will lose it; and whoever loses his life will gain it.

'I tell you, on that night there will be two people in one bed: one will be taken, the other left. There will be two women together grinding corn: one will be taken, the other left.' When they heard this they asked, 'Where, Lord?' He said, 'Where the carcass is, there will the vultures gather.'

The Parable of the Unjust Judge

He told them a parable to show that they should keep on praying and never lose heart: 'In a certain city there was a judge who had no fear of God or respect for man, and in the same city there was a widow who kept coming before him to demand justice against her opponent. For a time he refused; but in the end he said to himself, "Although I have no fear of God or respect for man, yet this widow is so great a nuisance that I will give her justice before she wears me out with her persistence."' The Lord said, 'You hear what the unjust judge says. Then will not God give justice to his chosen, to whom he listens patiently while they cry out to him day and night? I tell you, he will give them justice soon enough. But when the Son of Man comes, will he find faith on earth?'

The Parable of the Pharisee and the Tax-collector

Here is another parable that he told; it was aimed at those who were sure of their own goodness and looked down on everyone else. 'Two men went up to the temple to pray, one a Pharisee and the other a tax-collector. The Pharisee stood up and prayed this prayer: "I thank you, God, that I am not like the rest of mankind – greedy, dishonest, adulterous – or, for that matter, like this tax-collector. I fast twice a week; I pay tithes on all that I get." But the other kept his distance and would not even raise his eyes to heaven, but beat upon his breast, saying, "God, have mercy on me, sinner that I am." It was this man, I tell you, and not the other, who went home acquitted of his sins. For everyone who exalts himself will be humbled; and whoever humbles himself will be exalted.'

Jesus Blesses the Children

They brought children for him to touch. The disciples rebuked them, but when Jesus saw it he was indignant, and said to them, 'Let the children come to me; do not try to stop them; for the kingdom of God belongs to such as these. Truly I tell you: who-ever does not accept the kingdom of God like a child will never enter it.' And he put his arms round them, laid his hands on them, and blessed them.

The Rich Young Man

As he was starting out on a journey, a stranger ran up, and, kneel-ing before him, asked, 'Good Teacher, what must I do to win eternal life?' Jesus said to him, 'Why do you call me good? No one is good except God alone. You know the commandments: "Do not murder; do not commit adultery; do not steal; do not give false evidence; do not defraud; honour your father and mother."' 'But Teacher,' he replied, 'I have kept all these since I was a boy.' As Jesus looked at him, his heart warmed to him. 'One thing you lack,' he said. 'Go, sell everything you have, and give to the poor, and you will have treasure in heaven; then come and follow me.' At these words his face fell and he went away with a heavy heart; for he was a man of great wealth.

Many Who Are First Will Be Last

Jesus looked round at his disciples and said to them, 'How hard it will be for the wealthy to enter the kingdom of God!' They were amazed that he should say this, but Jesus insisted, 'Children, how hard it is to enter the kingdom of God! It is easier for a camel to pass through the eye of a needle than for a rich man to enter the kingdom of God.' They were more astonished than ever, and said to one another, 'Then who can be saved?' Jesus looked at them and said, 'For men it is impossible, but not for God; everything is possible for God.'

'What about us?' said Peter. 'We have left everything to follow you.' Jesus said, 'Truly I tell you: there is no one who has given up home, brothers or sisters, mother, father or children, or land, for my sake and for the gospel, who will not receive in this age a hundred times as much – houses, brothers and sisters, mothers and children, and land and persecutions besides; and in the age to come eternal life. But many who are first will be last, and the last first.'

James and John, the sons of Zebedee, approached him and said, 'Teacher, we should like you to do us a favour.' 'What is it you want me to do for you?' he asked. They answered, 'Allow us to sit with you in your glory, one at your right hand and the other at your left.' Jesus said to them, 'You do not understand what you are asking. Can you drink the cup that I drink, or be baptized with the baptism I am baptized with?' 'We can,' they answered. Jesus said, 'The cup that I drink you shall drink, and the baptism I am baptized with shall be your baptism; but to sit on my right or on my left is not for me to grant; that honour is for those to whom it has already been assigned.'

When the other ten heard this, they were indignant with James and John. Jesus called them to him and said, 'You know that among the Gentiles the recognized rulers lord it over their subjects, and the great make their authority felt. It shall not be so with you; among you, whoever wants to be great must be your servant, and whoever wants to be first must be the slave of all. For the Son of Man did not come to be served but to serve, and to give his life as a ransom for many.'

The Healing of a Blind Beggar

They came to Jericho; and as he was leaving the town, with his disciples and a large crowd, Bartimaeus (that is, son of Timaeus), a blind beggar, was seated at the roadside. Hearing that it was

Jesus of Nazareth, he began to shout, 'Son of David, Jesus, have pity on me!' Many of the people told him to hold his tongue; but he shouted all the more, 'Son of David, have pity on me.' Jesus stopped and said, 'Call him'; so they called the blind man: 'Take heart,' they said. 'Get up; he is calling you.' At that he threw off his cloak, jumped to his feet, and came to Jesus. Jesus said to him, 'What do you want me to do for you?' 'Rabbi,' the blind man answered, 'I want my sight back.' Jesus said to him, 'Go; your faith has healed you.' And at once he recovered his sight and followed him on the road.

Jesus and Zacchaeus

Entering Jericho he made his way through the city. There was a man there named Zacchaeus; he was superintendent of taxes and very rich. He was eager to see what Jesus looked like; but, being a little man, he could not see him for the crowd. So he ran on ahead and climbed a sycomore tree in order to see him, for he was to pass that way. When Jesus came to the place, he looked up and said, 'Zacchaeus, be quick and come down, for I must stay at your house today.' He climbed down as quickly as he could and welcomed him gladly. At this there was a general murmur of disapproval. 'He has gone in to be the guest of a sinner,' they said. But Zacchaeus stood there and said to the Lord, 'Here and now, sir, I give half my possessions to charity; and if I have defrauded anyone, I will repay him four times over.' Jesus said to him, 'Today salvation has come to this house, for this man too is a son of Abraham. The Son of Man has come to seek and to save what is lost.'

The Parable of the Money

While they were listening to this, he went on to tell them a parable, because he was now close to Jerusalem and they thought the kingdom of God might dawn at any moment. He said, 'A man of noble birth went on a long journey abroad, to have himself appointed king and then return. But first he called ten of his servants and gave them each a sum of money, saying, "Trade with this while I am away." His fellow citizens hated him and sent a delegation after him to say, "We do not want this man as our king." He returned however as king, and sent for the servants to whom he had given the money, to find out what profit each had made. The first came and said, "Your money, sir, has increased tenfold." "Well done," he replied; "you are a good servant. Because you have shown yourself trustworthy in a very small matter, you shall have charge of ten cities." The second came and said, "Your money, sir, has increased fivefold"; and he was told, "You shall be in charge of five cities." The third came and said, "Here is your money, sir; I kept it wrapped up in a handkerchief. I was afraid of you, because you are a hard man: you draw out what you did not put in and reap what you did not sow." "You scoundrel!" he replied. "I will condemn you out of your own mouth. You knew me to be a hard man, did you, drawing out what I never put in, and reaping what I did not sow? Then why did you not put my money on deposit, and I could have claimed it with interest when I came back?" Turning to his attendants he said, "Take the money from him and give it to the man with the most." "But, sir," they replied, "he has ten times as much already." "I tell you," he said, "everyone who has will be given more; but whoever has nothing will forfeit even what he has. But as for those enemies of mine who did not want me for their king, bring them here and slaughter them in my presence."'

The Parable of the Labourers in the Vineyard
'The kingdom of Heaven is like this. There was once a land owner who went out early one morning to hire labourers for his vineyard; and after agreeing to pay them the usual day's wage he sent them off to work. Three hours later he went out again and saw some more men standing idle in the market-place. "Go and join the others in the vineyard," he said, "and I will pay you a fair wage"; so off they went. At midday he went out again, and at three in the afternoon, and made the same arrangement as before. An hour

before sunset he went out and found another group standing there; so he said to them, "Why are you standing here all day doing nothing?" "Because no one has hired us," they replied; so he told them, "Go and join the others in the vineyard." When evening fell, the owner of the vineyard said to the overseer, "Call the labourers and give them their pay, beginning with those who came last and ending with the first." Those who had started work an hour before sunset came forward, and were paid the full day's wage. When it was the turn of the men who had come first, they expected something extra, but were paid the same as the others. As they took it, they grumbled at their employer: "These latecomers did only one hour's work, yet you have treated them on a level with us, who have sweated the whole day long in the blazing sun!" The owner turned to one of them and said, "My friend, I am not being unfair to you. You agreed on the usual wage for the day, did you not? Take your pay and go home. I choose to give the last man the same as you. Surely I am free to do what I like with my own money? Why be jealous because I am generous?" So the last will be first, and the first last.'

Jesus Causes a Division

Jesus went up to the temple and began to teach. The Jews were astonished: 'How is it', they said, 'that this untrained man has such learning?' Jesus replied, 'I was sent by one who is true, and him you do not know. I know him because I come from him, and he it is who sent me.' At this they tried to seize him, but no one could lay hands on him because his appointed hour had not yet come. Among the people many believed in him. 'When the Messiah comes,' they said, 'is it likely that he will perform more signs than this man?'

The Pharisees overheard these mutterings about him among the people, so the chief priests and the Pharisees sent temple police to arrest him. Then Jesus said, 'For a little longer I shall be with you; then I am going away to him who sent me. You will look for me, but you will not find me; and where I am, you cannot come.' So the Jews said to one another, 'Where does he intend to go, that we should not be able to find him? Will he go to the Dispersion among the Gentiles, and teach Gentiles? What does he mean by saying, "You will look for me, but you will not find me; and where I am, you cannot come"?'

On the last and greatest day of the festival Jesus stood and declared, 'If anyone is thirsty, let him come to me and drink. Whoever believes in me, as scripture says, "Streams of living water shall flow from within him."' He was speaking of the Spirit which believers in him would later receive; for the Spirit had not yet been given, because Jesus had not yet been glorified.

On hearing his words some of the crowd said, 'This must certainly be the Prophet.' Others said, 'This is the Messiah.' But others argued, 'Surely the Messiah is not to come from Galilee? Does not scripture say that the Messiah is to be of the family of David, from David's village of Bethlehem?' Thus he was the cause of a division among the people. Some were for arresting him, but no one laid hands on him.

The temple police went back to the chief priests and Pharisees, who asked them, 'Why have you not brought him?' 'No one ever spoke as this man speaks,' they replied. The Pharisees retorted, 'Have you too been misled? Has a single one of our rulers believed in him, or any of the Pharisees? As for this rabble, which cares nothing for the law, a curse is on them.' Then one of their number, Nicodemus (the man who once visited Jesus), intervened. 'Does our law', he asked them, 'permit us to pass judgement on someone without first giving him a hearing and learning the facts?' 'Are you a Galilean too?' they retorted. 'Study the scriptures and you will find that the Prophet does not come from Galilee.'

Jesus and the Woman Caught in Adultery

And they all went home, while Jesus went to the mount of Olives. At daybreak he appeared again in the temple, and all the people gathered round him. He had taken his seat and was engaged in teaching them when the scribes and the Pharisees brought in a woman caught committing adultery. Making her stand in the middle they said to him, 'Teacher, this woman was caught in the very act of adultery. In the law Moses has laid down that such women are to be stoned. What do you say about it?' They put the question as a test, hoping to frame a charge against him. Jesus bent down and wrote with his finger on the ground. When they continued to press their question he sat up straight and said, 'Let whichever of you is free from sin throw the first stone at her.' Then once again he bent down and wrote on the ground. When they heard what he said, one by one they went away, the eldest first; and Jesus was left alone, with the woman still standing there. Jesus again sat up and said to the woman, 'Where are they? Has no one condemned you?' She answered, 'No one, sir.' 'Neither do I condemn you,' Jesus said. 'Go; do not sin again.'

The Light of the World
Once again Jesus addressed the people: 'I am the light of the world. No follower of mine shall walk in darkness; he shall have the light of life.' The Pharisees said to him, 'You are witness in your own cause; your testimony is not valid.' Jesus replied, 'My testimony is valid, even though I do testify on my own behalf; because I know where I come from, and where I am going. But you know neither where I come from nor where I am going. I have much to say about you – and in judgement. But he who sent me speaks the truth, and what I heard from him I report to the world.'

They did not understand that he was speaking to them about the Father. So Jesus said to them, 'When you have lifted up the Son of Man you will know that I am what I am. I do nothing on my own authority, but in all I say, I have been taught by my Father. He who sent me is present with me, and has not left me on my own; for I always do what is pleasing to him.' As he said this, many put their faith in him.

The Truth Will Set You Free

Turning to the Jews who had believed him, Jesus said, 'If you stand by my teaching, you are truly my disciples; you will know the truth, and the truth will set you free.' 'We are Abraham's descendants,' they replied; 'we have never been in slavery to anyone. What do you mean by saying, "You will become free"?' 'In very truth I tell you', said Jesus, 'that everyone who commits sin is a slave. The slave has no permanent standing in the household, but the son belongs to it for ever. If then the Son sets you free, you will indeed be free.'

Before Abraham was Born, I am

'I know that you are descended from Abraham, yet you are bent on killing me because my teaching makes no headway with you. I tell what I have seen in my Father's presence. But because I speak the truth, you do not believe me. Which of you can convict me of sin? If what I say is true, why do you not believe me? He who has God for his father listens to the words of God. You are not God's children, and that is why you do not listen.'

The Jews answered, 'Are we not right in saying that you are a Samaritan, and that you are possessed?' 'I am not possessed,' said Jesus; 'I am honouring my Father, but you dishonour me. I do not care about my own glory; there is one who does care, and he is judge. In very truth I tell you, if anyone obeys my teaching he will never see death.'

The Jews said, 'Now we are certain that you are possessed. Abraham is dead and so are the prophets; yet you say, "If anyone obeys my teaching he will never taste death." Are you greater than our father Abraham? He is dead and the prophets too are dead. Who do you claim to be?'

Jesus replied, 'If I glorify myself, that glory of mine is worthless. It is the Father who glorifies me, he of whom you say, "He is our God," though you do not know him. But I know him; if I were to say that I did not know him I should be a liar like you. I do know him and I obey his word. Your father Abraham was overjoyed to see my day; he saw it and was glad.' The Jews protested, 'You are not yet fifty years old. How can you have seen Abraham?' Jesus said, 'In very truth I tell you, before Abraham was born, I am.' They took up stones to throw at him, but he was not to be seen; and he left the temple.

The Healing of a Man Born Blind

As he went on his way Jesus saw a man who had been blind from birth. His disciples asked him, 'Rabbi, why was this man born blind? Who sinned, this man or his parents?' 'It is not that he or his parents sinned,' Jesus answered; 'he was born blind so that God's power might be displayed in curing him. While daylight lasts we must carry on the work of him who sent me; night is coming, when no one can work. While I am in the world I am the light of the world.'

With these words he spat on the ground and made a paste with the spittle; he spread it on the man's eyes, and said to him, 'Go and wash in the pool of Siloam.' (The name means 'Sent'.) The man went off and washed, and came back able to see.

His neighbours and those who were accustomed to see him begging said, 'Is not this the man who used to sit and beg?' Some said, 'Yes, it is.' Others said, 'No, but it is someone like him.' He himself said, 'I am the man.' They asked him, 'How were your eyes opened?' He replied, 'The man called Jesus made a paste and smeared my eyes with it, and told me to go to Siloam and wash. So I went and washed, and found I could see.' 'Where is he?' they asked. 'I do not know,' he said.

The man who had been blind was brought before the Pharisees. As it was a sabbath day when Jesus made the paste and opened his eyes, the Pharisees too asked him how he had gained his sight. The man told them, 'He spread a paste on my eyes; then I washed, and now I can see.' Some of the Pharisees said, 'This man cannot be from God; he does not keep the sabbath.' Others said, 'How could such signs come from a sinful man?' So they took different sides. Then they continued to question him: 'What have you to say about him? It was your eyes he opened.' He answered, 'He is a prophet.'

The Jews would not believe that the man had been blind and had gained his sight, until they had summoned his parents and questioned them: 'Is this your son? Do you say that he was born blind? How is it that he can see now?' The parents replied, 'We know that he is our son, and that he was born blind. But how it is that he can now see, or who opened his eyes, we do not know. Ask him; he is of age; let him speak for himself.' His parents gave this answer because they were afraid of the Jews; for the Jewish authorities had already agreed that anyone who acknowledged Jesus as Messiah should be banned from the synagogue. That is why the parents said, 'He is of age; ask him.'

So for the second time they summoned the man who had been blind, and said, 'Speak the truth before God. We know that this man is a sinner.' 'Whether or not he is a sinner, I do not know,' the man replied. 'All I know is this: I was blind and now I can see.' 'What did he do to you?' they asked. 'How did he open your eyes?' 'I have told you already,' he retorted, 'but you took no notice. Why do you want to hear it again? Do you also want to become his disciples?' Then they became abusive. 'You are that man's disciple,' they said, 'but we are disciples of Moses. We know that God spoke to Moses, but as for this man, we do not know where he comes from.'

The man replied, 'How extraordinary! Here is a man who has opened my eyes, yet you do not know where he comes from! We know that God does not listen to sinners; he listens to anyone who is devout and obeys his will. To open the eyes of a man born blind – that is unheard of since time began. If this man was not from God he could do nothing.' 'Who are you to lecture us?' they retorted. 'You were born and bred in sin.' Then they turned him out.

Hearing that they had turned him out, Jesus found him and asked, 'Have you faith in the Son of Man?' The man answered, 'Tell me who he is, sir, that I may put my faith in him.' 'You have seen him,' said Jesus; 'indeed, it is he who is speaking to you.' 'Lord, I believe,' he said, and fell on his knees before him.

Jesus said, 'It is for judgement that I have come into this world – to give sight to the sightless and to make blind those who see.' Some Pharisees who were present asked, 'Do you mean that we are blind?' 'If you were blind,' said Jesus, 'you would not be guilty, but because you claim to see, your guilt remains.'

The Good Shepherd

'In very truth I tell you, the man who does not enter the sheep-fold by the door, but climbs in some other way, is nothing but a thief and a robber. He who enters by the door is the shepherd in charge of the sheep. The door-keeper admits him, and the sheep hear his voice; he calls his own sheep by name, and leads them out. When he has brought them all out, he goes ahead of them and the sheep follow, because they know his voice. They will not follow a stranger; they will run away from him, because they do not recognize the voice of strangers.

'A thief comes only to steal, kill, and destroy; I have come that they may have life, and may have it in all its fullness. I am the good shepherd; the good shepherd lays down his life for the sheep. The hired man, when he sees the wolf coming, abandons the sheep and runs away, because he is not the shepherd and the sheep are not his. Then the wolf harries the flock and scatters the sheep. The man runs away because he is a hired man and cares nothing for the sheep.

'I am the good shepherd; I know my own and my own know me, as the Father knows me and I know the Father; and I lay down my life for the sheep. But there are other sheep of mine, not belonging to this fold; I must lead them as well, and they too will listen to my voice. There will then be one flock, one shepherd. My Father who has given them to me is greater than all, and no one can snatch them out of the Father's care. The Father and I are one.'

This provoked them to make another attempt to seize him, but he escaped from their clutches.

The Raising of Lazarus

Jesus withdrew again across the Jordan, to the place where John had been baptizing earlier, and stayed there while crowds came to him. 'John gave us no miraculous sign,' they said, 'but all that he told us about this man was true.' And many came to believe in him there.

There was a man named Lazarus who had fallen ill. His home was at Bethany, the village of Mary and her sister Martha. This Mary, whose brother Lazarus had fallen ill, was the woman who anointed the Lord with ointment and wiped his feet with her hair. The sisters sent a message to him: 'Sir, you should know that your friend lies ill.' When Jesus heard this he said, 'This illness is not to end in death; through it God's glory is to be revealed and the Son of God glorified.' Therefore, though he loved Martha and her sister and Lazarus, he stayed where he was for two days after hearing of Lazarus's illness.

He then said to his disciples, 'Let us go back to Judaea.' 'Rabbi,' his disciples said, 'it is not long since the Jews there were wanting to stone you. Are you going there again?' Jesus replied, 'Are there not twelve hours of daylight? Anyone can walk in the daytime without stumbling, because he has this world's light to see by. But if he walks after nightfall he stumbles, because the light fails him.'

After saying this he added, 'Our friend Lazarus has fallen asleep, but I shall go and wake him.' The disciples said, 'Master, if he is sleeping he will recover.' Jesus had been speaking of Lazarus's death, but they thought that he meant natural sleep. Then Jesus told them plainly: 'Lazarus is dead. I am glad for your sake that I was not there; for it will lead you to believe. But let us go to him.' Thomas, called 'the Twin', said to his fellow disciples, 'Let us also go and die with him.'

On his arrival Jesus found that Lazarus had already been four days in the tomb. Bethany was just under two miles from Jerusalem, and many of the Jews had come from the city to visit Martha and Mary and condole with them about their brother. As soon as Martha heard that Jesus was on his way, she went to meet him, and left Mary sitting at home.

Martha said to Jesus, 'Lord, if you had been here my brother would not have died. Even now I know that God will grant you whatever you ask of him.' Jesus said, 'Your brother will rise again.' 'I know that he will rise again', said Martha, 'at the resurrection on the last day.' Jesus said, 'I am the resurrection and the life. Whoever has faith in me shall live, even though he dies; and no one who lives and has faith in me shall ever die. Do you believe this?' 'I do, Lord,' she answered; 'I believe that you are the Messiah, the Son of God who was to come into the world.'

So saying she went to call her sister Mary and, taking her aside, she said, 'The Master is here and is asking for you.' As soon as Mary heard this she rose and went to him. Jesus had not yet entered the village, but was still at the place where Martha had met him. When the Jews who were in the house condoling with Mary saw her hurry out, they went after her, assuming that she was going to the tomb to weep there.

Mary came to the place where Jesus was, and as soon as she saw him she fell at his feet and said, 'Lord, if you had been here my brother would not have died.' When Jesus saw her weeping and the Jews who had come with her weeping, he was moved with indignation and deeply distressed. 'Where have you laid him?' he asked. They replied, 'Come and see.' Jesus wept. The Jews said, 'How dearly he must have loved him!' But some of them said, 'Could not this man, who opened the blind man's eyes, have done something to keep Lazarus from dying?'

Jesus, again deeply moved, went to the tomb. It was a cave, with a stone placed against it. Jesus said, 'Take away the stone.' Martha, the dead man's sister, said to him, 'Sir, by now there will be a stench; he has been there four days.' Jesus said, 'Did I not tell you that if you have faith you will see the glory of God?' Then they removed the stone.

Jesus looked upwards and said, 'Father, I thank you for hearing me. I know that you always hear me, but I have spoken for the sake of the people standing round, that they may believe it was you who sent me.'

Then he raised his voice in a great cry: 'Lazarus, come out.' The dead man came out, his hands and feet bound with linen bandages, his face wrapped in a cloth. Jesus said, 'Loose him; let him go.'

The High Priest's Prophecy

Many of the Jews who had come to visit Mary, and had seen what Jesus did, put their faith in him. But some of them went off to the Pharisees and reported what he had done.

Thereupon the chief priests and the Pharisees convened a meeting of the Council. 'This man is performing many signs,' they said, 'and what action are we taking? If we let him go on like this the whole populace will believe in him, and then the Romans will come and sweep away our temple and our nation.' But one of them, Caiaphas, who was high priest that year, said, 'You have no grasp of the situation at all; you do not realize that it is more to your interest that one man should die for the people, than that the whole nation should be destroyed.' He did not say this of his own accord, but as the high priest that year he was prophesying that Jesus would die for the nation, and not for the nation alone but to gather together the scattered children of God. So from that day on they plotted his death.

6 | THE WAY TO THE CROSS

The Triumphal Entry

Jesus set out on the ascent to Jerusalem. As he approached Beth-phage and Bethany at the hill called Olivet, he sent off two of the disciples, telling them: 'Go into the village opposite; as you enter it you will find tethered there a colt which no one has yet ridden. Untie it and bring it here. If anyone asks why you are untying it, say, "The Master needs it."' The two went on their errand and found everything just as he had told them. As they were untying the colt, its owners asked, 'Why are you untying that colt?' They answered, 'The Master needs it.'

So they brought the colt to Jesus, and threw their cloaks on it for Jesus to mount. As he went along, people laid their cloaks on the road. And when he reached the descent from the mount of Olives, the whole company of his disciples in their joy began to sing aloud the praises of God for all the great things they had seen:

'Blessed is he who comes as king in the name of the Lord!
Peace in heaven, glory in highest heaven!'

Some Pharisees in the crowd said to him, 'Teacher, restrain your disciples.' He answered, 'I tell you, if my disciples are silent the stones will shout aloud.'

When he came in sight of the city, he wept over it and said, 'If only you had known this day the way that leads to peace! But no; it is hidden from your sight. For a time will come upon you, when your enemies will set up siege-works against you; they will encircle you and hem you in at every point; they will bring you to the ground, you and your children within your walls, and not leave you one stone standing on another, because you did not recognize the time of God's visitation.'

The Cleansing of the Temple

He entered Jerusalem and went into the temple. He looked round at everything; then, as it was already late, he went out to Bethany with the Twelve.

On the following day, as they left Bethany, he felt hungry, and, noticing in the distance a fig tree in leaf, he went to see if he could find anything on it. But when he reached it he found nothing but leaves; for it was not the season for figs. He said to the tree, 'May no one ever again eat fruit from you!' And his disciples were listening.

So they came to Jerusalem, and he went into the temple and began to drive out those who bought and sold there. He upset the tables of the money-changers and the seats of the dealers in pigeons; and he would not allow anyone to carry goods through the temple court. Then he began to teach them, and said, 'Does not scripture say, "My house shall be called a house of prayer for all nations"? But you have made it a robbers' cave.' The chief priests and the scribes heard of this and looked for a way to bring about his death; for they were afraid of him, because the whole crowd was spellbound by his teaching. And when evening came they went out of the city.

Early next morning, as they passed by, they saw that the fig tree had withered from the roots up; and Peter, recalling what had happened, said to him, 'Rabbi, look, the fig tree which you cursed has withered.' Jesus answered them, 'Have faith in God. Truly I tell you: if anyone says to this mountain, "Be lifted from your place and hurled into the sea," and has no inward doubts, but believes that what he says will happen, it will be done for him. I tell you, then, whatever you ask for in prayer, believe that you have received it and it will be yours.'

A Question of Authority

He entered the temple, and, as he was teaching, the chief priests and elders of the nation came up to him and asked: 'By what authority are you acting like this? Who gave you this authority?' Jesus replied, 'I also have a question for you. If you answer it, I will tell you by what authority I act. The baptism of John: was it from God, or from men?' This set them arguing among themselves: 'If we say, "From God," he will say, "Then why did you not believe him?" But if we say, "From men," we are afraid of the people's reaction, for they all take John for a prophet.' So they answered, 'We do not know.' And Jesus said: 'Then I will not tell you either by what authority I act.'

The Parable of the Two Sons

'But what do you think about this? There was a man who had two sons. He went to the first, and said, "My son, go and work today in the vineyard." "I will, sir," the boy replied; but he did not go. The father came to the second and said the same. "I will not," he replied; but afterwards he changed his mind and went. Which of the two did what his father wanted?' 'The second,' they replied. Then Jesus said, 'Truly I tell you: tax-collectors and prostitutes are entering the kingdom of God ahead of you. For when John came to show you the right way to live, you did not believe him, but the tax-collectors and prostitutes did; and even when you had seen that, you did not change your minds and believe him.'

The Parable of the Wicked Tenants

'Listen to another parable. There was a landowner who planted a vineyard: he put a wall round it, hewed out a winepress, and built a watch-tower; then he let it out to vine-growers and went abroad. When the harvest season approached, he sent his servants to the tenants to collect the produce due to him. But they seized his servants, thrashed one, killed another, and stoned a third. Again, he sent other servants, this time a larger number; and they treated them in the same way. Finally he sent his son. "They will respect my son," he said. But when they saw the son the tenants said to one another, "This is the heir; come on, let us kill him, and get his inheritance." So they seized him, flung him out of the vineyard, and killed him. When the owner of the vineyard comes, how do you think he will deal with those tenants?' 'He will bring those bad men to a bad end,' they answered, 'and hand the vineyard over to other tenants, who will give him his share of the crop when the season comes.' Jesus said to them, 'Have you never read in the scriptures: "The stone which the builders rejected has become the main corner-stone. This is the Lord's doing, and it is wonderful in our eyes"? Therefore, I tell you, the kingdom of God will be taken away from you, and given to a nation that yields the proper fruit.'

When the chief priests and Pharisees heard his parables, they saw that he was referring to them. They wanted to arrest him, but were afraid of the crowds, who looked on Jesus as a prophet.

The Parable of the Wedding Banquet

Jesus spoke to them again in parables: 'The kingdom of Heaven is like this. There was a king who arranged a banquet for his son's wedding; but when he sent his servants to summon the guests he had invited, they refused to come. Then he sent other servants, telling them to say to the guests, "Look! I have prepared this banquet for you. My bullocks and fatted beasts have been slaughtered, and everything is ready. Come to the wedding." But they took no notice; one went off to his farm, another to his business, and the others seized the servants, attacked them brutally, and killed them. The king was furious; he sent troops to put those murderers to death and set their town on fire. Then he said to his servants, "The wedding banquet is ready; but the guests I invited did not deserve the honour. Go out therefore to the main thoroughfares, and invite everyone you can find to the wedding." The servants went out into the streets, and collected everyone they could find, good and bad alike. So the hall was packed with guests.

'When the king came in to watch them feasting, he observed a man who was not dressed for a wedding. "My friend," said the king, "how do you come to be here without wedding clothes?" But he had nothing to say. The king then said to his attendants, "Bind him hand and foot; fling him out into the dark, the place of wailing and grinding of teeth." For many are invited, but few are chosen.'

Pay Caesar What Belongs to Caesar

A number of Pharisees and men of Herod's party were sent to trap him with a question. They came and said, 'Teacher, we know you are a sincere man and court no one's favour, whoever he may be; you teach in all sincerity the way of life that God requires. Are we or are we not permitted to pay taxes to the Roman emperor? Shall we pay or not?' He saw through their duplicity, and said, 'Why are you trying to catch me out? Fetch me a silver piece, and let me look at it.' They brought one, and he asked them, 'Whose head is this, and whose inscription?' 'Caesar's,' they replied. Then Jesus said, 'Pay Caesar what belongs to Caesar, and God what belongs to God.' His reply left them completely taken aback.

A Question About the Resurrection

Next Sadducees, who maintain that there is no resurrection, came to him and asked: 'Teacher, Moses laid it down for us that if there are brothers, and one dies leaving a wife but no child, then the next should marry the widow and provide an heir for his brother. Now there were seven brothers. The first took a wife and died without issue. Then the second married her, and he too died without issue; so did the third; none of the seven left any issue. Finally the woman died. At the resurrection, when they rise from the dead, whose wife will she be, since all seven had married her?' Jesus said to them, 'How far you are from the truth! You know neither the scriptures nor the power of God. When they rise from the dead, men and women do not marry; they are like angels in heaven.

'As for the resurrection of the dead, have you not read in the book of Moses, in the story of the burning bush, how God spoke to him and said, "I am the God of Abraham, the God of Isaac, the God of Jacob"? He is not God of the dead but of the living. You are very far from the truth.'

The Two Great Commandments

Then one of the scribes, who had been listening to these discussions and had observed how well Jesus answered, came forward and asked him, 'Which is the first of all the commandments?' He answered, 'The first is, "Hear, O Israel: the Lord our God is the one Lord, and you must love the Lord your God with all your heart, with all your soul, with all your mind, and with all your strength." The second is this: "You must love your neighbour as yourself." No other commandment is greater than these.' The scribe said to him, 'Well said, Teacher. You are right in saying that God is one and beside him there is no other. And to love him with all your heart, all your understanding, and all your strength, and to love your neighbour as yourself – that means far more than any whole-offerings and sacrifices.' When Jesus saw how thoughtfully he answered, he said to him, 'You are not far from the kingdom of God.'

A Question About David's Son

Turning to the assembled Pharisees Jesus asked them, 'What is your opinion about the Messiah? Whose son is he?' 'The son of David,' they replied. 'Then how is it', he asked, 'that David by inspiration calls him "Lord"? For he says, "The Lord said to my Lord, 'Sit at my right hand until I put your enemies under your feet.'" If then David calls him "Lord", how can he be David's son?' Nobody was able to give him an answer; and from that day no one dared to put any more questions to him.

The Widow's Penny

As he was sitting opposite the temple treasury, he watched the people dropping their money into the chest. Many rich people were putting in large amounts. Presently there came a poor widow who dropped in two tiny coins, together worth a penny. He called his disciples to him and said, 'Truly I tell you: this poor widow has given more than all those giving to the treasury; for the others who have given had more than enough, but she, with less than enough, has given all that she had to live on.'

Warnings About the End

As he was leaving the temple, one of his disciples exclaimed, 'Look, Teacher, what huge stones! What fine buildings!' Jesus said to him, 'You see these great buildings? Not one stone will be left upon another; they will all be thrown down.'

As he sat on the mount of Olives opposite the temple he was questioned privately by Peter, James, John, and Andrew. 'Tell us,' they said, 'when will this happen? What will be the sign that all these things are about to be fulfilled?'

Jesus began: 'Be on your guard; let no one mislead you. Many will come claiming my name, and saying, "I am he"; and many will be misled by them. When you hear of wars and rumours of wars, do not be alarmed. Such things are bound to happen; but the end is still to come. For nation will go to war against nation, kingdom against kingdom; there will be earthquakes in many places; there will be famines. These are the first birth-pangs of the new age.

'As for you, be on your guard. You will be handed over to the courts; you will be beaten in synagogues; you will be summoned to appear before governors and kings on my account to testify in their presence. Before the end the gospel must be proclaimed to all nations. So when you are arrested and put on trial do not worry beforehand about what you will say, but when the time comes say whatever is given you to say, for it is not you who will be speaking, but the Holy Spirit. Brother will hand over brother to death, and a father his child; children will turn against their parents and send them to their death. Everyone will hate you for your allegiance to me, but whoever endures to the end will be saved.

'But when you see "the abomination of desolation" usurping a place which is not his (let the reader understand), then those who are in Judaea must take to the hills. If anyone is on the roof, he must not go down into the house to fetch anything out; if anyone is in the field, he must not turn back for his coat. Alas for women with child in those days, and for those who have children at the breast! Pray that it may not come in winter. For those days will bring distress such as there has never been before since the beginning of the world which God created, and will never be again. If the Lord had not cut short that time of troubles, no living thing could survive. However, for the sake of his own, whom he has chosen, he has cut short the time.

'If anyone says to you then, "Look, here is the Messiah," or, "Look, there he is," do not believe it. Impostors will come claiming to be messiahs or prophets, and they will produce signs and wonders to mislead, if possible, God's chosen. Be on your guard; I have forewarned you of it all.

'But in those days, after that distress,
the sun will be darkened,
the moon will not give her light;
the stars will come falling from the sky,
the celestial powers will be shaken.

'Then they will see the Son of Man coming in the clouds with great power and glory, and he will send out the angels and gather his chosen from the four winds, from the farthest bounds of earth to the farthest bounds of heaven.

'Learn a lesson from the fig tree. When its tender shoots appear and are breaking into leaf, you know that summer is near. In the same way, when you see all this happening, you may know that the end is near, at the very door. Truly I tell you: the present generation will live to see it all. Heaven and earth will pass away, but my words will never pass away. Yet about that day or hour no one knows, not even the angels in heaven, not even the Son; no one but the Father.

'Be on your guard, keep watch. You do not know when the moment is coming. It is like a man away from home: he has left his house and put his servants in charge, each with his own work to do, and he has ordered the door-keeper to stay awake. Keep awake, then, for you do not know when the master of the house will come. Evening or midnight, cock-crow or early dawn – if he comes suddenly, do not let him find you asleep. And what I say to you, I say to everyone: Keep awake.'

The Parable of the Good and Bad Servants
'Who is the faithful and wise servant, charged by his master to manage his household and supply them with food at the proper time? Happy that servant if his master comes home and finds him at work! Truly I tell you: he will be put in charge of all his master's property. But if he is a bad servant and says to himself, "The master is a long time coming," and begins to bully the other servants and to eat and drink with his drunken friends, then the master will arrive on a day when the servant does not expect him, at a time he has not been told. He will cut him in pieces and assign him a place among the hypocrites, where there is wailing and grinding of teeth.'

The Parable of the Ten Girls
'When the day comes, the kingdom of Heaven will be like this. There were ten girls, who took their lamps and went out to meet the bridegroom. Five of them were foolish, and five prudent; when the foolish ones took their lamps, they took no oil with them, but the others took flasks of oil with their lamps. As the bridegroom was a long time in coming, they all dozed off to sleep. But at midnight there came a shout: "Here is the bridegroom!

Come out to meet him." Then the girls all got up and trimmed their lamps. The foolish said to the prudent, "Our lamps are going out; give us some of your oil." "No," they answered; "there will never be enough for all of us. You had better go to the dealers and buy some for yourselves." While they were away the bridegroom arrived; those who were ready went in with him to the wedding banquet; and the door was shut. Later the others came back. "Sir, sir, open the door for us," they cried. But he answered, "Truly I tell you: I do not know you." Keep awake then, for you know neither the day nor the hour.'

The Parable of the Sheep and the Goats

'When the Son of Man comes in his glory and all the angels with him, he will sit on his glorious throne, with all the nations gathered before him. He will separate people into two groups, as a shepherd separates the sheep from the goats; he will place the sheep on his right hand and the goats on his left. Then the king will say to those on his right, "You have my Father's blessing; come, take possession of the kingdom that has been ready for you since the world was made. For when I was hungry, you gave me food; when thirsty, you gave me drink; when I was a stranger, you took me into your home; when naked, you clothed me; when I was ill, you came to my help; when in prison, you visited me." Then the righteous will reply, "Lord, when was it that we saw you hungry and fed you, or thirsty and gave you drink, a stranger and took you home, or naked and clothed you? When did we see you ill or in prison, and come to visit you?" And the king will answer, "Truly I tell you: anything you did for one of my brothers here, however insignificant, you did for me." Then he will say to those on his left, "A curse is on you; go from my sight to the eternal fire that is ready for the devil and his angels. For when I was hungry, you gave me nothing to eat; when thirsty, nothing to drink; when I was a stranger, you did not welcome me; when I was naked, you did not clothe me; when I was ill and in prison, you did not come to my help." And they in their turn will reply,

"Lord, when was it that we saw you hungry or thirsty or a stranger or naked or ill or in prison, and did nothing for you?" And he will answer, "Truly I tell you: anything you failed to do for one of these, however insignificant, you failed to do for me." And they will go away to eternal punishment, but the righteous will enter eternal life.'

7 | PASSION AND RESURRECTION

The Chief Priests Plot Against Jesus

When Jesus had finished all these discourses he said to his disciples, 'You know that in two days' time it will be Passover, when the Son of Man will be handed over to be crucified.'

Meanwhile the chief priests and the elders of the people met in the house of the high priest, Caiaphas, and discussed a scheme to seize Jesus and put him to death. 'It must not be during the festival,' they said, 'or there may be rioting among the people.'

The Anointing at Bethany

Jesus was at Bethany in the house of Simon the leper, when a woman approached him with a bottle of very costly perfume; and she began to pour it over his head as he sat at table. The disciples were indignant when they saw it. 'Why this waste?' they said. 'It could have been sold for a large sum and the money given to the poor.' Jesus noticed, and said to them, 'Why make trouble for the woman? It is a fine thing she has done for me. You have the poor among you always, but you will not always have me. When she poured this perfume on my body it was her way of preparing me for burial. Truly I tell you: wherever this gospel is proclaimed throughout the world, what she has done will be told as her memorial.'

Jesus Anticipates his Death

Among those who went up to worship at the festival were some Gentiles. They approached Philip, who was from Bethsaida in Galilee, and said to him, 'Sir, we should like to see Jesus.' Philip went and told Andrew, and the two of them went to tell Jesus. Jesus replied: 'The hour has come for the Son of Man to be glorified. In very truth I tell you, unless a grain of wheat falls into the ground and dies, it remains that and nothing more; but if it dies, it bears a rich harvest. Whoever loves himself is lost, but he who hates himself in this world will be kept safe for eternal life. If anyone is to serve me, he must follow me; where I am, there will my servant be. Whoever serves me will be honoured by the Father.

'Now my soul is in turmoil, and what am I to say? "Father, save me from this hour"? No, it was for this that I came to this hour. Father, glorify your name.' A voice came from heaven: 'I have glorified it, and I will glorify it again.' The crowd standing by said it was thunder they heard, while others said, 'An angel has spoken to him.' Jesus replied, 'This voice spoke for your sake, not mine. Now is the hour of judgement for this world; now shall the prince of this world be driven out. And when I am lifted up from the earth I shall draw everyone to myself.' This he said to indicate the kind of death he was to die.

The Last Supper

Then one of the Twelve, the man called Judas Iscariot, went to the chief priests and said, 'What will you give me to betray him to you?' They weighed him out thirty silver pieces. From that moment he began to look for an opportunity to betray him.

On the first day of Unleavened Bread the disciples came and asked Jesus, 'Where would you like us to prepare the Passover for you?' He told them to go to a certain man in the city with this message: 'The Teacher says, "My appointed time is near; I shall keep the Passover with my disciples at your house."' The disciples did as Jesus directed them and prepared the Passover.

During supper, Jesus, well aware that the Father had entrusted everything to him, and that he had come from God and was going back to God, rose from the supper table, took off his outer garment and, taking a towel, tied it round him. Then he poured water into a basin, and began to wash his disciples' feet and to wipe them with the towel.

When he came to Simon Peter, Peter said to him, 'You, Lord, washing my feet?' Jesus replied, 'You do not understand now what I am doing, but one day you will.' Peter said, 'I will never let you wash my feet.' 'If I do not wash you,' Jesus replied, 'you have no part with me.' 'Then, Lord,' said Simon Peter, 'not my feet only; wash my hands and head as well!'

Jesus said to him, 'Anyone who has bathed needs no further washing; he is clean all over; and you are clean, though not every one of you.' He added the words 'not every one of you' because he knew who was going to betray him.

After washing their feet he put on his garment and sat down again. 'Do you understand what I have done for you?' he asked. 'You call me Teacher and Lord, and rightly so, for that is what I am. Then if I, your Lord and Teacher, have washed your feet, you also ought to wash one another's feet. I have set you an example: you are to do as I have done for you. In very truth I tell you, a servant is not greater than his master, nor a messenger than the one who sent him. If you know this, happy are you if you act upon it.

'I am not speaking about all of you; I know whom I have chosen. But there is a text of scripture to be fulfilled: "He who eats bread with me has turned against me." I tell you this now, before the event, so that when it happens you may believe that I am what I am. In very truth I tell you, whoever receives any messenger of mine receives me; and receiving me, he receives the One who sent me.'

After saying this, Jesus exclaimed in deep distress, 'In very truth I tell you, one of you is going to betray me.' The disciples looked at one another in bewilderment: which of them could he mean? One of them, the disciple he loved, was reclining close beside Jesus. Simon Peter signalled to him to find out which one he meant. That disciple leaned back close to Jesus and asked, 'Lord, who is it?' Jesus replied, 'It is the one to whom I give this piece of bread when I have dipped it in the dish.' Then he took it, dipped it in the dish, and gave it to Judas son of Simon Iscariot. As soon as Judas had received it, Satan entered him. Jesus said to him, 'Do quickly what you have to do.' No one at the table understood what he meant by this. Some supposed that, as Judas was in charge of the common purse, Jesus was telling him to buy what was needed for the festival, or to make some gift to the poor. As soon as Judas had received the bread he went out. It was night.

During supper Jesus took bread, and having said the blessing he broke it and gave it to the disciples with the words: 'Take this and eat; this is my body.' Then he took a cup, and having offered thanks to God he gave it to them with the words: 'Drink from it, all of you. For this is my blood, the blood of the covenant, shed for many for the forgiveness of sins. I tell you, never again shall I drink from this fruit of the vine until that day when I drink it new with you in the kingdom of my Father.'

After singing the Passover hymn, they went out to the mount of Olives. Then Jesus said to them, 'Tonight you will all lose faith because of me; for it is written: "I will strike the shepherd and the sheep of his flock will be scattered." But after I am raised, I shall go ahead of you into Galilee.' Peter replied, 'Everyone else may lose faith because of you, but I never will.' Jesus said to him, 'Truly I tell you: tonight before the cock crows you will disown me three times.'

The Way, the Truth and the Life

'Set your troubled hearts at rest. Trust in God always; trust also in me. There are many dwelling-places in my Father's house; if it were not so I should have told you; for I am going to prepare a place for you. And if I go and prepare a place for you, I shall come again and take you to myself, so that where I am you may be also; and you know the way I am taking.' Thomas said, 'Lord, we do not know where you are going, so how can we know the way?' Jesus replied, 'I am the way, the truth, and the life; no one comes to the Father except by me.

'If you knew me you would know my Father too. From now on you do know him; you have seen him.' Philip said to him, 'Lord, show us the Father; we ask no more.' Jesus answered, 'Have I been all this time with you, Philip, and still you do not know me? Anyone who has seen me has seen the Father.'

The Gift of Peace
'Peace is my parting gift to you, my own peace, such as the world cannot give. Set your troubled hearts at rest, and banish your fears. You heard me say, "I am going away, and I am coming back to you." If you loved me you would be glad that I am going to the Father; for the Father is greater than I am. I have told you now, before it happens, so that when it does happen you may have faith.

'I shall not talk much longer with you, for the prince of this world approaches. He has no rights over me; but the world must be shown that I love the Father and am doing what he commands.'

The True Vine
'I am the true vine, and my Father is the gardener. Any branch of mine that is barren he cuts away; and any fruiting branch he prunes clean, to make it more fruitful still. You are already clean because of the word I have spoken to you. Dwell in me, as I in you. No branch can bear fruit by itself, but only if it remains united with the vine; no more can you bear fruit, unless you remain united with me.

'I am the vine; you are the branches. Anyone who dwells in me, as I dwell in him, bears much fruit; apart from me you can do nothing. Anyone who does not dwell in me is thrown away like a withered branch. The withered branches are gathered up, thrown on the fire, and burnt.

'If you dwell in me, and my words dwell in you, ask whatever you want, and you shall have it. This is how my Father is glorified: you are to bear fruit in plenty and so be my disciples. As the

Father has loved me, so I have loved you. Dwell in my love. If you heed my commands, you will dwell in my love, as I have heeded my Father's commands and dwell in his love.'

Love One Another

'I have spoken thus to you, so that my joy may be in you, and your joy complete. This is my commandment: love one another, as I have loved you. There is no greater love than this, that someone should lay down his life for his friends. You are my friends, if you do what I command you. No longer do I call you servants, for a servant does not know what his master is about. I have called you friends, because I have disclosed to you everything that I heard from my Father. You did not choose me: I chose you. I appointed you to go on and bear fruit, fruit that will last; so that the Father may give you whatever you ask in my name. This is my commandment to you: love one another.'

The Spirit of Truth

'There is much more that I could say to you, but the burden would be too great for you now. However, when the Spirit of truth comes, he will guide you into all the truth; for he will not speak on his own authority, but will speak only what he hears; and he will make known to you what is to come. He will glorify me, for he will take what is mine and make it known to you. All that the Father has is mine, and that is why I said, "He will take what is mine and make it known to you."'

Sorrow and Joy

'In very truth I tell you, you will weep and mourn, but the world will be glad. But though you will be plunged in grief, your grief will be turned to joy. A woman in labour is in pain because her time has come; but when her baby is born she forgets the anguish in her joy that a child has been born into the world. So it is with you: for the moment you are sad; but I shall see you again, and then you will be joyful, and no one shall rob you of your joy.

'I have told you all this so that in me you may find peace. In the world you will have suffering. But take heart! I have conquered the world.'

Jesus Prays for his Disciples

Then Jesus looked up to heaven and said: 'Father, the hour has come. Glorify your Son, that the Son may glorify you. For you have made him sovereign over all mankind, to give eternal life to all whom you have given him. This is eternal life: to know you – the only true God, and Jesus Christ whom you have sent.

'I have glorified you on earth by finishing the work which you gave me to do; and now, Father, glorify me in your own presence with the glory which I had with you before the world began.

'I have made your name known to the men whom you gave me out of the world. They were yours and you gave them to me, and they have obeyed your command. Now they know that all you gave me has come from you; for I have taught them what I learned from you, and they have received it.

'It is not for these alone that I pray, but for those also who through their words put their faith in me. May they all be one; as you, Father, are in me, and I in you, so also may they be in us, that the world may believe that you sent me.'

The Agony in the Garden

When they reached a place called Gethsemane, he said to his disciples, 'Sit here while I pray.' And he took Peter and James and John with him. Horror and anguish overwhelmed him, and he said to them, 'My heart is ready to break with grief; stop here, and stay awake.' Then he went on a little farther, threw himself on the ground, and prayed that if it were possible this hour might pass him by. 'Abba, Father,' he said, 'all things are possible to you; take this cup from me. Yet not my will but yours.'

He came back and found them asleep; and he said to Peter, 'Asleep, Simon? Could you not stay awake for one hour? Stay awake, all of you; and pray that you may be spared the test. The spirit is willing, but the flesh is weak.' Once more he went away and prayed. On his return he found them asleep again, for their eyes were heavy; and they did not know how to answer him.

He came a third time and said to them, 'Still asleep? Still resting? Enough! The hour has come. The Son of Man is betrayed into the hands of sinners. Up, let us go! The traitor is upon us.'

While he was still speaking a crowd appeared with the man called Judas, one of the Twelve, at their head. He came up to Jesus to kiss him; but Jesus said, 'Judas, would you betray the Son of Man with a kiss?'

When his followers saw what was coming, they said, 'Lord, shall we use our swords?' And one of them struck at the high priest's servant, cutting off his right ear. But Jesus answered, 'Stop! No more of that!' Then he touched the man's ear and healed him.

Turning to the chief priests, the temple guards, and the elders, who had come to seize him, he said, 'Do you take me for a robber, that you have come out with swords and cudgels? Day after day, I have been with you in the temple, and you did not raise a hand against me. But this is your hour – when darkness reigns.'

Peter Denies Jesus

Then they arrested him and led him away. They brought him to the high priest's house, and Peter followed at a distance. They lit a fire in the middle of the courtyard and sat round it, and Peter sat among them. A serving-maid who saw him sitting in the firelight stared at him and said, 'This man was with him too.' But he denied it: 'I do not know him,' he said. A little later a man noticed him and said, 'You also are one of them.' But Peter said to him, 'No, I am not.' About an hour passed and someone else spoke more strongly still: 'Of course he was with him. He must have been; he is a Galilean.' But Peter said, 'I do not know what you are talking about.' At that moment, while he was still speaking, a cock crowed; and the Lord turned and looked at Peter. Peter remembered the Lord's words, 'Tonight before the cock crows you will disown me three times.' And he went outside, and wept bitterly.

The Trial Before the High Priest

The chief priests and the whole Council tried to find some allegation against Jesus that would warrant a death sentence; but they failed to find one, though many came forward with false evidence. Finally two men alleged that he had said, 'I can pull down the temple of God, and rebuild it in three days.' At this the high priest rose and said to him, 'Have you no answer to the accusations that these witnesses bring against you?' But Jesus remained silent. The high priest then said, 'By the living God I charge you to tell us: are you the Messiah, the Son of God?' Jesus replied, 'The words are yours. But I tell you this: from now on you will see the Son of Man seated at the right hand of the Almighty and coming on the clouds of heaven.' At these words the high priest tore his robes and exclaimed, 'This is blasphemy! Do we need further witnesses? You have just heard the blasphemy. What is your verdict?' 'He is guilty,' they answered; 'he should die.'

Then they spat in his face and struck him with their fists; some said, as they beat him, 'Now, Messiah, if you are a prophet, tell us who hit you.'

When Judas the traitor saw that Jesus had been condemned, he was seized with remorse, and returned the thirty silver pieces to the chief priests and elders. 'I have sinned,' he said; 'I have brought an innocent man to his death.' But they said, 'What is that to us? It is your concern.' So he threw the money down in the temple and left; he went away and hanged himself.

The Trial Before Pilate

From Caiaphas Jesus was led into the governor's headquarters. It was now early morning, and the Jews themselves stayed outside the headquarters to avoid defilement, so that they could eat the Passover meal. So Pilate came out to them and asked, 'What charge do you bring against this man?' 'If he were not a criminal', they replied, 'we would not have brought him before you.' Pilate said, 'Take him yourselves and try him by your own law.' The Jews answered, 'We are not allowed to put anyone to death.'

Thus they ensured the fulfilment of the words by which Jesus had indicated the kind of death he was to die.

Pilate then went back into his headquarters and summoned Jesus. 'So you are the king of the Jews?' he said. Jesus replied, 'Is that your own question, or have others suggested it to you?' 'Am I a Jew?' said Pilate. 'Your own nation and their chief priests have brought you before me. What have you done?' Jesus replied, 'My kingdom does not belong to this world. If it did, my followers would be fighting to save me from the clutches of the Jews. My kingdom belongs elsewhere.' 'You are a king, then?' said Pilate. Jesus answered, '"King" is your word. My task is to bear witness to the truth. For this I was born; for this I came into the world, and all who are not deaf to truth listen to my voice.' Pilate said, 'What is truth?'

Jesus is Sent to Herod

Pilate then said to the chief priests and the crowd, 'I find no case for this man to answer.' But they insisted: 'His teaching is causing unrest among the people all over Judaea. It started from Galilee and now has spread here.'

When Pilate heard this, he asked if the man was a Galilean, and on learning that he belonged to Herod's jurisdiction he remitted the case to him, for Herod was also in Jerusalem at that time. When Herod saw Jesus he was greatly pleased; he had heard about him and had long been wanting to see him in the hope of witnessing some miracle performed by him. He questioned him at some length without getting any reply; but the chief priests and scribes appeared and pressed the case against him vigorously. Then Herod and his troops treated him with contempt and ridicule, and sent him back to Pilate dressed in a gorgeous robe. That same day Herod and Pilate became friends; till then there had been a feud between them.

Pilate Washes his Hands of Jesus
Pilate now summoned the chief priests, councillors, and people, and said to them, 'You brought this man before me on a charge of subversion. But, as you see, I have myself examined him in your presence and found nothing in him to support your charges. No more did Herod, for he has referred him back to us. Clearly he has done nothing to deserve death. I therefore propose to flog him and let him go.'

At the festival season it was customary for the governor to release one prisoner chosen by the people. There was then in custody a man of some notoriety, called Jesus Barabbas. When the people assembled, Pilate said to them, 'Which would you like me to release to you – Jesus Barabbas, or Jesus called Messiah?' For he knew it was out of malice that Jesus had been handed over to him.

While Pilate was sitting in court a message came to him from his wife: 'Have nothing to do with that innocent man; I was much troubled on his account in my dreams last night.'

Meanwhile the chief priests and elders had persuaded the crowd to ask for the release of Barabbas and to have Jesus put to death. So when the governor asked, 'Which of the two would you like me to release to you?' they said, 'Barabbas.' 'Then what am I to do with Jesus called Messiah?' asked Pilate; and with one voice they answered, 'Crucify him!' 'Why, what harm has he done?' asked Pilate; but they shouted all the louder, 'Crucify him!'

When Pilate saw that he was getting nowhere, and that there was danger of a riot, he took water and washed his hands in full view of the crowd. 'My hands are clean of this man's blood,' he declared. 'See to that yourselves.'

Jesus is Flogged and Condemned to Death
Pilate now took Jesus and had him flogged; and the soldiers plaited a crown of thorns and placed it on his head, and robed him in a purple cloak. Then one after another they came up to him, crying, 'Hail, king of the Jews!' and struck him on the face.

Once more Pilate came out and said to the Jews, 'Here he is; I am bringing him out to let you know that I find no case against him'; and Jesus came out, wearing the crown of thorns and the purple cloak. 'Here is the man,' said Pilate. At the sight of him the chief priests and the temple police shouted, 'Crucify! Crucify!' 'Take him yourselves and crucify him,' said Pilate; 'for my part I find no case against him.' The Jews answered, 'We have a law; and according to that law he ought to die, because he has claimed to be God's Son.'

When Pilate heard that, he was more afraid than ever, and going back into his headquarters he asked Jesus, 'Where have you come from?' But Jesus gave him no answer. 'Do you refuse to speak to me?' said Pilate. 'Surely you know that I have authority to release you, and authority to crucify you?' 'You would have no authority at all over me', Jesus replied, 'if it had not been granted you from above; and therefore the deeper guilt lies with the one who handed me over to you.'

From that moment Pilate tried hard to release him; but the Jews kept shouting, 'If you let this man go, you are no friend to Caesar; anyone who claims to be a king is opposing Caesar.' When Pilate heard what they were saying, he brought Jesus out and took his seat on the tribunal at the place known as The Pavement (in Hebrew, 'Gabbatha'). It was the day of preparation for the Passover, about noon. Pilate said to the Jews, 'Here is your king.' They shouted, 'Away with him! Away with him! Crucify him!' 'Am I to crucify your king?' said Pilate. 'We have no king but Caesar,' replied the chief priests. Then at last, to satisfy them, he handed Jesus over to be crucified.

The Crucifixion

As they led him away to execution they took hold of a man called Simon, from Cyrene, on his way in from the country; putting the cross on his back they made him carry it behind Jesus.

Great numbers of people followed, among them many women who mourned and lamented over him. Jesus turned to them and said, 'Daughters of Jerusalem, do not weep for me; weep for yourselves and your children. For the days are surely coming when people will say, "Happy are the barren, the wombs that never bore a child, the breasts that never fed one." Then they will begin to say to the mountains, "Fall on us," and to the hills, "Cover us." For if these things are done when the wood is green, what will happen when it is dry?'

There were two others with him, criminals who were being led out to execution; and when they reached the place called The Skull, they crucified him there, and the criminals with him, one on his right and the other on his left. Jesus said, 'Father, forgive them; they do not know what they are doing.'

Pilate had an inscription written and fastened to the cross; it read, 'Jesus of Nazareth, King of the Jews'. This inscription, in Hebrew, Latin, and Greek, was read by many Jews, since the place where Jesus was crucified was not far from the city. So the Jewish chief priests said to Pilate, 'You should not write "King of the Jews", but rather "He claimed to be king of the Jews".' Pilate replied, 'What I have written, I have written.'

When the soldiers had crucified Jesus they took his clothes and, leaving aside the tunic, divided them into four parts, one for each soldier. The tunic was seamless, woven in one piece throughout; so they said to one another, 'We must not tear this; let us toss for it.' Thus the text of scripture came true: 'They shared my garments among them, and cast lots for my clothing.'

That is what the soldiers did. Meanwhile near the cross on which Jesus hung, his mother was standing with her sister, Mary wife of Clopas, and Mary of Magdala. Seeing his mother, with the disciple whom he loved standing beside her, Jesus said to her, 'Mother, there is your son'; and to the disciple, 'There is your mother'; and from that moment the disciple took her into his home.

The passers-by wagged their heads and jeered at him, crying, 'So you are the man who was to pull down the temple and rebuild it in three days! If you really are the Son of God, save yourself and come down from the cross.' The chief priests with the scribes and elders joined in the mockery: 'He saved others,' they said, 'but he cannot save himself. King of Israel, indeed! Let him come down now from the cross, and then we shall believe him. He trusted in God, did he? Let God rescue him, if he wants him – for he said he was God's Son.'

One of the criminals hanging there taunted him: 'Are not you the Messiah? Save yourself, and us.' But the other rebuked him: 'Have you no fear of God? You are under the same sentence as he is. In our case it is plain justice; we are paying the price for our misdeeds. But this man has done nothing wrong.' And he said, 'Jesus, remember me when you come to your throne.' Jesus answered, 'Truly I tell you: today you will be with me in Paradise.'

From midday a darkness fell over the whole land, which lasted until three in the afternoon; and about three Jesus cried aloud, '*Eli, Eli, lema sabachthani?*' which means, 'My God, my God, why have you forsaken me?' Hearing this, some of the bystanders said, 'He is calling Elijah.'

After this, Jesus, aware that all had now come to its appointed end, said in fulfilment of scripture, 'I am thirsty.' A jar stood there full of sour wine; so they soaked a sponge with the wine, fixed it on hyssop, and held it up to his lips. Having received the wine, he said, 'It is accomplished!'

Then Jesus uttered a loud cry and said, 'Father, into your hands I commit my spirit'; and with these words he died.

At that moment the curtain of the temple was torn in two from top to bottom. The earth shook, rocks split, and graves opened; many of God's saints were raised from sleep, and coming out of their graves after his resurrection entered the Holy City, where many saw them. And when the centurion and his men who were keeping watch over Jesus saw the earthquake and all that was happening, they were filled with awe and said, 'This must have been a son of God.'

Because it was the eve of the sabbath, the Jews were anxious that the bodies should not remain on the crosses, since that sabbath was a day of great solemnity; so they requested Pilate to have the legs broken and the bodies taken down. The soldiers accordingly came to the men crucified with Jesus and broke the legs of each in turn, but when they came to Jesus and found he was already dead, they did not break his legs. But one of the soldiers thrust a lance into his side, and at once there was a flow of blood and water. This is vouched for by an eyewitness, whose evidence is to be trusted. He knows that he speaks the truth, so that you too may believe; for this happened in fulfilment of the text of scripture: 'No bone of his shall be broken.' And another text says, 'They shall look on him whom they pierced.'

After that, Joseph of Arimathaea, a disciple of Jesus, but a secret disciple for fear of the Jews, asked Pilate for permission to remove the body of Jesus. He consented; so Joseph came and removed the body. He was joined by Nicodemus (the man who had visited Jesus by night), who brought with him a mixture of myrrh and aloes, more than half a hundredweight. They took the body of Jesus and following Jewish burial customs they wrapped it, with the spices, in strips of linen cloth. Near the place where he had been crucified there was a garden, and in the garden a new tomb, not yet used for burial; and there, since it was the eve of the Jewish sabbath and the tomb was near at hand, they laid Jesus.

The Resurrection

Early on the first day of the week, while it was still dark, Mary of Magdala came to the tomb. She saw that the stone had been moved away from the entrance, and ran to Simon Peter and the other disciple, the one whom Jesus loved. 'They have taken the Lord out of the tomb,' she said, 'and we do not know where they have laid him.' So Peter and the other disciple set out and made their way to the tomb. They ran together, but the other disciple ran faster than Peter and reached the tomb first. He peered in and saw the linen wrappings lying there, but he did not enter. Then Simon Peter caught up with him and went into the tomb. He saw the linen wrappings lying there, and the napkin which had been round his head, not with the wrappings but rolled up in a place by itself. Then the disciple who had reached the tomb first also went in, and he saw and believed; until then they had not understood the scriptures, which showed that he must rise from the dead.

So the disciples went home again; but Mary stood outside the tomb weeping. And as she wept, she peered into the tomb, and saw two angels in white sitting there, one at the head, and one at the feet, where the body of Jesus had lain. They asked her, 'Why are you weeping?' She answered, 'They have taken my Lord away, and I do not know where they have laid him.' With these words she turned round and saw Jesus standing there, but she did not recognize him. Jesus asked her, 'Why are you weeping? Who are you looking for?' Thinking it was the gardener, she said, 'If it is you, sir, who removed him, tell me where you have laid him, and I will take him away.' Jesus said, 'Mary!' She turned and said to him, 'Rabbuni!' (which is Hebrew for 'Teacher'). 'Do not cling to me,' said Jesus, 'for I have not yet ascended to the Father. But go to my brothers, and tell them that I am ascending to my Father and your Father, to my God and your God.' Mary of Magdala went to tell the disciples. 'I have seen the Lord!' she said, and gave them his message.

The Supper at Emmaus
That same day two of them were on their way to a village called Emmaus, about seven miles from Jerusalem, talking together about all that had happened. As they talked and argued, Jesus himself came up and walked with them; but something prevented them from recognizing him. He asked them, 'What is it you are debating as you walk?' They stood still, their faces full of sadness, and one, called Cleopas, answered, 'Are you the only person staying in Jerusalem not to have heard the news of what has happened there in the last few days?' 'What news?' he said. 'About Jesus of Nazareth,' they replied, 'who, by deeds and words of power, proved himself a prophet in the sight of God and the whole people; and how our chief priests and rulers handed him over to be sentenced to death, and crucified him. But we had been hoping that he was to be the liberator of Israel.'

'How dull you are!' he answered. 'How slow to believe all that the prophets said! Was not the Messiah bound to suffer in this way before entering upon his glory?' Then, starting from Moses and all the prophets, he explained to them in the whole of scripture the things that referred to himself.

By this time they had reached the village to which they were going, and he made as if to continue his journey. But they pressed him: 'Stay with us, for evening approaches, and the day is almost over.' So he went in to stay with them. And when he had sat down with them at table, he took bread and said the blessing; he broke the bread, and offered it to them. Then their eyes were opened, and they recognized him; but he vanished from their sight. They said to one another, 'Were not our hearts on fire as he talked with us on the road and explained the scriptures to us?'

Without a moment's delay they set out and returned to Jerusalem. There they found that the eleven and the rest of the company had assembled. Then they described what had happened on their journey and told how he had made himself known to them in the breaking of the bread.

Doubting Thomas
As they were talking about all this, there he was, standing among them. Startled and terrified, they thought they were seeing a ghost. But he said, 'Why are you so perturbed? Why do doubts arise in your minds? Look at my hands and feet. It is I myself. Touch me and see; no ghost has flesh and bones as you can see that I have.' They were still incredulous, still astounded, for it seemed too good to be true. So he asked them, 'Have you anything here to eat?' They offered him a piece of fish they had cooked, which he took and ate before their eyes.

And he said to them, 'This is what I meant by saying, while I was still with you, that everything written about me in the law of Moses and in the prophets and psalms was bound to be fulfilled.' Then he opened their minds to understand the scriptures. 'So you see', he said, 'that scripture foretells the sufferings of the Messiah and his rising from the dead on the third day, and declares that in his name repentance bringing the forgiveness of sins is to be proclaimed to all nations beginning from Jerusalem. You are to be witnesses to it all. I am sending on you the gift promised by my Father. As the Father sent me, so I send you.' Then he breathed on them, saying, 'Receive the Holy Spirit! If you forgive anyone's sins, they are forgiven; if you pronounce them unforgiven, unforgiven they remain.'

One of the Twelve, Thomas the Twin, was not with the rest when Jesus came. So the others kept telling him, 'We have seen the Lord.' But he said, 'Unless I see the mark of the nails on his hands, unless I put my finger into the place where the nails were, and my hand into his side, I will never believe it.'

A week later his disciples were once again in the room, and Thomas was with them. Although the doors were locked, Jesus came and stood among them, saying, 'Peace be with you!' Then he said to Thomas, 'Reach your finger here; look at my hands. Reach your hand here and put it into my side. Be unbelieving no longer, but believe.' Thomas said, 'My Lord and my God!' Jesus said to him, 'Because you have seen me you have found faith. Happy are they who find faith without seeing me.'

The Great Commission
The eleven disciples made their way to Galilee, to the mountain where Jesus had told them to meet him. When they saw him, they knelt in worship, though some were doubtful. Jesus came near and said to them: 'Full authority in heaven and on earth has been committed to me. Go therefore to all nations and make them my disciples; baptize them in the name of the Father and the Son and the Holy Spirit, and teach them to observe all that I have commanded you. I will be with you always, to the end of time.'

Follow Me

Some time later, Jesus showed himself to his disciples once again, by the sea of Tiberias. This is how it happened. Simon Peter was with Thomas the Twin, Nathanael from Cana-in-Galilee, the sons of Zebedee, and two other disciples. 'I am going out fishing,' said Simon Peter. 'We will go with you,' said the others. So they set off and got into the boat; but that night they caught nothing.

Morning came, and Jesus was standing on the beach, but the disciples did not know that it was Jesus. He called out to them, 'Friends, have you caught anything?' 'No,' they answered. He said, 'Throw out the net to starboard, and you will make a catch.' They did so, and found they could not haul the net on board, there were so many fish in it. Then the disciple whom Jesus loved said to Peter, 'It is the Lord!' As soon as Simon Peter heard him say, 'It is the Lord,' he fastened his coat about him (for he had stripped) and plunged into the sea. The rest of them came on in the boat, towing the net full of fish. They were only about a hundred yards from land.

When they came ashore, they saw a charcoal fire there with fish laid on it, and some bread. Jesus said, 'Bring some of the fish you have caught.' Simon Peter went on board and hauled the net to land; it was full of big fish, a hundred and fifty-three in all; and yet, many as they were, the net was not torn. Jesus said, 'Come and have breakfast.' None of the disciples dared to ask 'Who are you?' They knew it was the Lord.

After breakfast Jesus said to Simon Peter, 'Simon son of John, do you love me more than these others?' 'Yes, Lord,' he answered, 'you know that I love you.' 'Then feed my lambs,' he said. A second time he asked, 'Simon son of John, do you love me?' 'Yes, Lord, you know I love you.' 'Then tend my sheep.' A third time he said, 'Simon son of John, do you love me?' Peter was hurt that he asked him a third time, 'Do you love me?' 'Lord,' he said, 'you know everything; you know I love you.' Jesus said, 'Then feed my sheep.

'In very truth I tell you: when you were young you fastened your belt about you and walked where you chose; but when you are old you will stretch out your arms, and a stranger will bind you fast, and carry you where you have no wish to go.' He said this to indicate the manner of death by which Peter was to glorify God.

Then he added, 'Follow me.'

NOTES TO PART ONE

1 *Jewish War* 2.164–5.
2 *Inferno* xxii.82.
3 Some scholars are disputing this essential claim of Jacob Neusner, say for instance in his *Judaism in the Beginning of Christianity* (Philadelphia: Fortress, 1984), 45–61. For an alternative view, see E. P. Sanders, *Judaism: Practice and Belief 63 BCE–66 CE* (Philadelphia: Trinity Press International, 1992), 380–451.
4 This creed, at least in later times, became a collection of texts, and not just Deuteronomy 6:4–8. It also included, perhaps, the Ten Commandments from either Exodus 20 or Deuteronomy 6, as well as texts from Deuteronomy 11:13–21 and Numbers 15:37–41.
5 *Freedom, Fame, Lying, and Betrayal* (Boulder: Westview, 1999), 7.
6 Even here, a more literal translation makes the saying more radical: 'unless your righteousness far exceeds that of the scribes and Pharisees'.
7 William Hazlitt, *Selected Essays* (ed. J. R. Nabholz; Chicago: Loyola, 1970), 1.
8 *I Saw Satan Fall Like Lightning* (Maryknoll, NY: Orbis, 2004).
9 A good survey can be found in R. E. Brown, *The Birth of the Messiah* (ABRL; Garden City, NY: Doubleday, 1993), 350–65. See my study of Mary in *The Jesus Creed*, ch. 8.
10 This prayer can be studied in Rabbi L. A. Hoffman, *The* Amidah (My People's Prayer Book: Traditional Prayers, Modern Commentaries, Volume 2; Woodstock, Vermont: Jewish Lights, 1998).
11 *Orthodoxy: The Romance of Faith* (New York: Doubleday, 1990), 95.
12 *The Autobiography of G. K. Chesterton* (San Francisco: Ignatius, 1988), 116.
13 *The Autobiography of Benjamin Franklin* (New York: Barnes and Noble, 1994), 23.
14 *The Years with Ross* (Boston: Little, Brown, 1959), 57.
15 *The Complete Works* (New York: A. A. Knopf, 2003), 58.

16 Jane Austen, *Sense and Sensibility* (New York: Dover, 1996), 79.
17 *Collected Works* (New York: Library of America, 1988), 1035.
18 C. S. Lewis, *Collected Letters: Volume 1: Family Letters 1905–1931* (ed. W. Hooper; London: HarperCollins, 2000), 772.
19 Samuel Johnson, *Selected Essays* from the *Rambler, Adventurer*, and *Idler* (ed. W. J. Bate; New Haven: Yale, 1968), 101 (from #47, 28 August 1750, Tuesday).
20 Rowan Williams, *The Wound of Knowledge: Christian Spirituality from the New Testament to Saint John of the Cross* (Cambridge, Massachusetts: Cowley, 1990), 23–4.
21 *Walden, or Life in the Woods* (New York: A. A. Knopf, 1992), 7.
22 See G. B. Caird, *New Testament Theology* (completed by L. D. Hurst; Oxford: OUP, 1994), 380.
23 *The Everlasting Man* (San Francisco: Ignatius, 1993), 192–3.

INDEX OF GOSPEL SOURCES

	Source	*Page*
1. Birth and Early Years		
Prologue	John 1	64
The Angel Gabriel Appears to Zechariah	Luke 1	65
The Annunciation of the Birth of Jesus	Luke 1	66
Joseph's Dream	Matthew 1	67
Mary Visits Elizabeth	Luke 1	67
The Magnificat	Luke 1	67
The Birth of John the Baptist	Luke 1	68
The Birth of Jesus	Luke 2/Matthew 2	69
The Flight into Egypt	Luke 2/Matthew 2	72
The Boy Jesus in the Temple	Luke 2	73
2. Baptism and Early Ministry		
John the Baptist	Luke 3	74
The Baptism of Jesus	Matthew 3	75
The Temptations	Luke 4	75
The First Disciples	John 1	76
The Marriage at Cana	John 2	77
The First Journey to Jerusalem	John 2	78
Jesus and Nicodemus	John 3	78
Jesus and the Samaritan Woman	John 4	79
Jesus Teaches in the Synagogue at Nazareth	Luke 4	81
The First Healings	Luke 4	82
The Miraculous Catch of Fish	Luke 5	83
The Cleansing of a Leper	Mark 1	83
The Healing of a Paralysed Man	Mark 2	84
The Call of Levi	Mark 2	84
New Wine in Old Wine Skins	Mark 2	85
Lord of the Sabbath	Mark 2	85
The Healing of a Man with the Withered Hand	Luke 6	86
The Twelve Disciples	Luke 6	86
Blessings and Warnings	Luke 6	86
The Healing of a Centurion's Servant	Luke 7	87
The Raising of a Widow's Son	Luke 7	88

	Source	*Page*
The Parable of the Sower	Mark 4	88
Two Parables of the Kingdom	Mark 4	89
The Calming of the Storm	Mark 4	90
The Healing of a Madman	Mark 5	90
The Healing of Jairus's Daughter and of a Woman		
who Suffered from Haemorrhages	Mark 5	91
3. The Sermon on the Mount		
The Beatitudes	Matthew 5	93
Salt and Light	Matthew 5	94
The Completion of the Law	Matthew 5	94
The Spirit of the Law	Matthew 5	94
Love Without Limits	Matthew 5	96
True Religion	Matthew 6	96
Do Not be Anxious	Matthew 6	98
Do Not Judge	Matthew 7	98
Concluding Teachings	Matthew 7	98
4. Healings and Teachings		
Jesus Commissions the Twelve Disciples	Matthew 10	101
Jesus Teaches in Nearby Towns	Matthew 11	103
Jesus Commends John the Baptist	Luke 7	103
A Woman Anoints Jesus's Feet	Luke 7	105
The Women who Followed Jesus	Luke 8	106
Jesus Denounces the Pharisees	Matthew 12	106
Brothers of Jesus	Matthew 12	107
The Parable of the Wheat and the Darnel	Matthew 13	108
More Parables of the Kingdom	Matthew 13	109
The Beheading of John the Baptist	Mark 6	109
The Healing at the Pool of Bethesda	John 5	110
The Feeding of the Five Thousand	John 6	112
Jesus Walks on Water	Matthew 14	112
The Bread of Life	John 6	113
The Meaning of Defilement	Mark 7	114
Jesus and the Syro-Phoenician Woman	Mark 7	115
The Healing of a Deaf Man	Mark 7	116
The Healing of a Blind Man	Mark 8	116
Peter's Confession	Matthew 16	117
Jesus Foretells his Passion	Matthew 16	117
The Transfiguration	Mark 9	118
The Healing of a Boy Possessed by a Spirit	Mark 9	118
Paying the Temple Tax	Matthew 17	119
The Greatest in the Kingdom	Matthew 18	119
Reproof and Reconciliation	Matthew 18	120
The Parable of the Unmerciful Servant	Matthew 18	120
Not One of Us	Luke 9	121

	Source	Page
5. The Road to Jerusalem		
No Looking Back	Luke 9	122
Jesus Commissions More Disciples	Luke 10	122
The Parable of the Good Samaritan	Luke 10	123
In the House of Mary and Martha	Luke 10	124
The Parable of the Persistent Friend	Luke 11	124
Warnings Against the Pharisees	Luke 11	124
The Parable of the Rich Fool	Luke 12	125
The Need for Repentance	Luke 13	126
The Parable of the Barren Fig Tree	Luke 13	126
The Healing of a Crippled Woman	Luke 13	126
A Warning Against Herod	Luke 13	127
The Healing of a Man with Dropsy	Luke 14	127
The Need for Humility	Luke 14	128
The Parable of the Great Banquet	Luke 14	128
The Cost of Discipleship	Luke 14	129
The Parable of the Lost Sheep	Luke 15	129
The Parable of the Lost Coin	Luke 15	130
The Parable of the Prodigal Son	Luke 15	130
The Parable of the Unjust Steward	Luke 16	131
On Divorce and Celibacy	Matthew 19	132
The Parable of the Rich Man and Lazarus	Luke 16	133
The Parable of the Dutiful Servants	Luke 17	133
The Cleansing of Ten Lepers	Luke 17	134
The Day of the Son of Man	Luke 17	134
The Parable of the Unjust Judge	Luke 18	135
The Parable of the Pharisee and the Tax-Collector	Luke 18	135
Jesus Blesses the Children	Mark 10	136
The Rich Young Man	Mark 10	136
Many Who Are First Will Be Last	Mark 10	136
The Healing of a Blind Beggar	Mark 10	137
Jesus and Zacchaeus	Luke 19	138
The Parable of the Money	Luke 19	138
The Parable of the Labourers in the Vineyard	Matthew 20	139
Jesus Causes a Division	John 7	140
Jesus and the Woman Caught in Adultery	John 8	141
The Light of the World	John 8	142
The Truth Will Set You Free	John 8	143
Before Abraham was Born, I am	John 8	143
The Healing of a Man Born Blind	John 9	144
The Good Shepherd	John 10	146
The Raising of Lazarus	John 11	147
The High Priest's Prophecy	John 11	149

	Source	*Page*
6. The Way to the Cross		
The Triumphal Entry	Luke 19	150
The Cleansing of the Temple	Mark 11	151
A Question of Authority	Matthew 21	152
The Parable of the Two Sons	Matthew 21	152
The Parable of the Wicked Tenants	Matthew 21	152
The Parable of the Wedding Banquet	Matthew 22	153
Pay Caesar What Belongs to Ceasar	Mark 12	154
A Question About the Resurrection	Mark 12	154
The Two Great Commandments	Mark 12	155
A Question About David's Son	Matthew 22	155
The Widow's Penny	Mark 12	156
Warnings About the End	Mark 13	156
The Parable of the Good and Bad Servants	Matthew 24	158
The Parable of the Ten Girls	Matthew 25	158
The Parable of the Sheep and the Goats	Matthew 25	159
7. Passion and Resurrection		
The Chief Priests Plot Against Jesus	Matthew 26	161
The Anointing at Bethany	Matthew 26	161
Jesus Anticipates his Death	John 12	161
The Last Supper	Matthew 26/John 13	162
The Way, the Truth and the Life	John 14	164
The Gift of Peace	John 14	165
The True Vine	John 15	165
Love One Another	John 15	166
The Spirit of Truth	John 16	166
Sorrow and Joy	John 16	166
Jesus Prays for his Disciples	John 17	167
The Agony in the Garden	Mark 14/Luke 22	167
Peter Denies Jesus	Luke 22	168
The Trial Before the High Priest	Matthew 26–27	169
The Trial Before Pilate	John 18	169
Jesus is Sent to Herod	Luke 23	170
Pilate Washes his Hands of Jesus	Luke 23/Matthew 27	171
Jesus is Flogged and Condemned to Death	John 19	171
The Crucifixion	Luke 23/John 19/	
	Matthew 27	172
The Resurrection	John 20	175
The Supper at Emmaus	Luke 24	176
Doubting Thomas	Luke 24/John 20	177
The Great Commission	Matthew 28	178
Follow Me	John 21	179